ar
e 6

ger Gower

CUSTOMER SERVICE EXCELLENCE

Libraries & Archives

Kent
County
Council

00884\DTP\RN\07.07   LIB 7

with tests

MBRIDGE
VERSITY PRESS

CAMBRIDGE UNIVERSITY PRESS
Cambridge, New York, Melbourne, Madrid, Cape Town, Singapore, São Paulo

Cambridge University Press
The Edinburgh Building, Cambridge CB2 2RU, UK

www.cambridge.org
Information on this title: www.cambridge.org/9780521618298

First published 2006
Reprinted 2006

Printed in Italy by Legoprint S.p.A.

A catalogue record for this publication is available from the British Library

ISBN -13 978-0-521-61829-8 paperback
ISBN -10 0-521-61829-0 paperback

Contents

1 I've been thinking

Continuous and perfect forms

We use continuous forms:
- to talk about temporary events over a period of time. **I'm staying** with friends at the moment.
- to focus on the action/situation and to emphasise 'how long'. He **was cooking** dinner all afternoon.
- to show a situation is changing/developing. He **was getting** stronger every day.

ⓘ State verbs (*like, seem, think, have*) are not normally used in the continuous. When these verbs are used in the continuous they suggest a temporary activity: **I'm thinking** of changing jobs. (considering)

We use perfect forms to link an earlier action with a later situation:
- to talk about an action which happened before another action. When I arrived, she **had already eaten**.
- for actions/states that began earlier and continue to a later time. **I've lived** here **for** years/**since** 1998 and I'm still here. (*for* = period of time; *since* = a specific time)
- to talk about the result of an earlier action. Look! **I've found** the bracelet that I lost.

ⓘ With perfect forms, the exact time that something happened is not important.

ⓘ We often combine the continuous and perfect. He **had been** reading.

A Underline the correct answer.

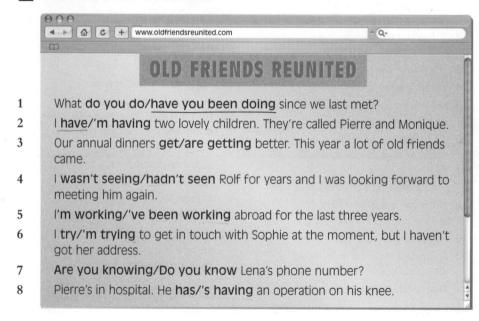

OLD FRIENDS REUNITED

1 What **do you do/have you been doing** since we last met?

2 I **have/'m having** two lovely children. They're called Pierre and Monique.

3 Our annual dinners **get/are getting** better. This year a lot of old friends came.

4 I **wasn't seeing/hadn't seen** Rolf for years and I was looking forward to meeting him again.

5 I'm **working/'ve been working** abroad for the last three years.

6 I **try/'m trying** to get in touch with Sophie at the moment, but I haven't got her address.

7 **Are you knowing/Do you know** Lena's phone number?

8 Pierre's in hospital. He **has/'s having** an operation on his knee.

B Correct the mistakes in these sentences.

1 'How are you? I <u>don't see</u> you for ages.' *haven't seen*
  'No, we<u>'re not meeting</u> since 2002.' ....

2 'Do you know Germany well?'
  'Yes, I<u>'m going</u> there many times in recent years.' ....

3 By the time I got to the party, all my friends <u>were leaving</u>. I didn't know anyone.
  ....

4 'I <u>just find</u> Paul's email address. Do you want it?' ....

5 'How long <u>do you know</u> Julia?' ....
  'We<u>'re</u> friends for years. We see each other at least once a week.' ....

6 I called Maria last week. Before that I <u>wasn't speaking</u> to her for ages.
  ....

C Write the verbs in the continuous, the perfect or the perfect continuous in this magazine article.

MY LIFE AS A MODEL

When I started at school, the other children
<u>*were always laughing*</u> (1 always/laugh) at me
because I was shorter than they were and not very pretty.
By the time I left school, however, I ....
(2 grow) a lot and was the tallest girl in my class.

A few years later, I .... (3 study) law
at university when a friend suggested that I took up
modelling. I was amazed because, before then,
I .... (4 never/think) of myself as very
attractive, but she disagreed. Like many of my university
friends, she .... (5 have to) get a
part-time job and .... (6 work) in the evenings as a part-time model
for one of the big agencies. When I left university, I decided to join her.

Since then, I .... (7 work) as a fashion model and I love it.
I .... (8 travel) all over the world for the big fashion magazines – 48
countries in all! – and I .... (9 have) many wonderful experiences.

Recently, though, I .... (10 read) the autobiography of a famous
model. She writes about the difficulties faced by older models and now
I .... (11 get) more anxious about the future. Should I change my
career? I .... (12 always/like) the idea of acting and at the moment
I .... (13 think) of having lessons. Sometimes I regret that
I .... (14 never/take) the time to practise law!

2 I had my car repaired

	need	+ *-ing*/passive infinitive
The windows	**need**	**cleaning.** **to be cleaned.**

have/get	+ object	+ past participle
Have you **had**	**your hair**	**cut**? (Did someone else cut your hair?)
I want to **get**	**the house**	**redecorated.** (*get* is usually more informal)

ⓘ We can also use *have/get something done* when someone does something to us we don't want. **I had my passport stolen.** (*had* = not my fault) **I got my coat caught** in the door of the car.

A Renata has bought a new house. Use *need* or *have/get something done* and complete her conversation with the agent.

1 'The central heating <u>needs repairing/</u>
<u>to be repaired.</u>'
'OK, I'll have it repaired.'

2 'The front door ....?'
'Don't worry. I'll get it painted.'

3 'The kitchen needs cleaning.'
'Really? OK, I'll ....?'

4 'The garden ....?'
'Right. I'll get it tidied.'

5 'Some lights need to be fitted.'
'Do they? OK, I'll ....?'

6 'The bedrooms ....?'
'OK, I'll have them decorated.'

B Which of these sentences are true for you? Underline the true sentences.

1 **I clean my car/I have my car cleaned** when it's dirty.

2 **I paint my room/I get my room painted** when it needs decorating.

3 **I mend the TV/I get the TV mended** when it's broken.

4 **I cut my hair/I have my hair cut** when it's long.

5 On one occasion **I stole some money/I had some money stolen**.

3 You must remember

Modal verbs

We use modal verbs to talk about
- ability: I **can't** see you now – I'm busy. He **could** play the guitar when he was seven.
- certainty: It**'ll** rain tomorrow. You **must** know him – he lives next door. He **can't** be 60 – he looks too young.
- obligation and necessity: We **ought to/should** phone and let them know. I really **must** go. All passengers **must** wear seat belts.
- permission: **Could/Can** I borrow some money? **May/Can** I leave early?
- possibility: Be careful with those glasses – you **could** drop them. I **might** be late. It **can** get very hot in this house. She **should** be here soon. (I expect she will be)
- prohibition: You **mustn't** talk here. Be quiet! You **can't** drive yet – you're too young.

ⓘ We use modals when we request something (**Could** you open the window, please? **Will** you lend me your coat?) and when we make an offer or suggestion (I**'ll** help you. **Shall** we take a picnic?).

ⓘ Affirmative: I **might** stay. NOT I ~~might to stay~~. Question: **Must** I go? NOT ~~Do I must ...~~? Negative: I **shouldn't** leave. NOT I ~~don't should~~.

A Underline the correct answer.

Evelyn Glennie is a world-famous percussionist. As she is 80% deaf and (1) **can't/mustn't** hear sounds clearly, she performs barefoot so that she (2) **should/can** feel the vibrations of her instruments and the orchestra. This (3) **should/must** be very difficult for her but she insists that people (4) **shouldn't/couldn't** take any notice of her disability and only judge her by how well she performs. When Evelyn left school she (5) **might/could** already play the clarinet, harmonica and snare drum but at first she (6) **mustn't/couldn't** get a place in a music college because of her deafness. After her great success, she believes that everyone with her disability (7) **should/can** be given the chance to pursue a musical career if they wish. As well as being a great musician, Evelyn (8) **may/can** also draw and paint.

B Use the most likely modal verb to complete these sentences. There might be more than one possible answer.

1 People *should/ought to* listen to classical music more often. It can be very exciting.

2 Do you think we .... get tickets today, or will it be OK to buy them at the door?

3 The performance starts at 8.00 pm so you .... be late or you won't get in.

4 Tell Katie she absolutely .... turn off her mobile phone before the concert starts.

5 '............................ we take photographs during the show?'
'No, sorry, you .... ?'

6 Do you think you .... go and get me some water? I'm thirsty.

C Complete the gaps with a positive or negative modal and a verb from the box.

| agree | be | continue | cure | get | give | ~~perform~~ | use |

Tonight's show cancelled!

The great singer has lost her voice and (1) *can't perform* on stage tonight. Her producers say that she (2) .... better in time for tomorrow's performance either. However, they're hoping that the medicine (3) .... her throat infection and that her schedule (4) .... as normal after that. If you have tickets for tonight's show, you (5) .... a refund by returning them to the box office sometime tomorrow. However, the singer (6) .... to return at the end of her tour and give an extra concert, in which case you (7) .... the same tickets. The singer has promised that she (8) .... her decision later today.

D Rewrite the sentences with a modal.

1 I'm sure it's going to rain. It's got very dark in the last few minutes.
It must be going to rain . It's got very dark in the last few minutes.

2 It's possible I'll go out later. I'm bored sitting at home.
.... I'm bored sitting at home.

3 I'm sure my friends are wondering where I am.
.... where I am.

4 I don't believe this is the right road. We're lost.
.... We're lost.

4 They'd been working

Narrative tenses

We use the past simple to talk about:
- completed actions/situations in the past. He **lived** in Tokyo when he was a child.
- actions which happened quickly one after the other. I **came in, sat down** and **fell** asleep.
- repeated actions/situations (often with a frequency adverb). They **went** to the beach **every summer**.

ⓘ We can use *would* for habits or *used to* for habits/states. He **would** often go out. I **used to** live by the sea.

We use the past continuous for longer actions/events and background descriptions. We **were working** last Tuesday. She **was wearing** a heavy overcoat.

We use the past perfect to talk about actions/situations in the past which happened before another action in the past. When they got to the station the train **had** already **left**.

We use the past perfect continuous to talk about an action that went on over a period of time before a past time. They**'d been waiting** an hour before she arrived.

ⓘ If the order of events is clear we often prefer the past simple to the past perfect. The train **left** before we got there.

A Write the verb in the most likely narrative tense.

```
File  Edit  View  Favorites  Tools  Help
Back  →  ⊙ ⊡ ⌂  Search  Favorites  Media  ⊙  ⊟ ⊜ ⊠ ⊟
Address
                                                         Go  Links »
```

Our Travel Blog

1 We _were driving_ (drive) to Denver when Hali _started_ (start) to feel sick.

2 When we .... (get) to Bogota, we were tired because we .... (travel) for six hours.

3 I .... (reach) the top of the hill, ... (look) at the map and .... (realise) that I was a long way from the city.

4 It was July and our August trip to Britain .... (get) closer. We .... (plan) the trip since January and as the months .... (go) by we .... (start) to feel nervous.

5 Raisa .... (walk) down the mountain when her foot .... (go) into a hole. She .... (shout) and .... (be) in great pain because she .... (break) her ankle.

B Underline the correct verb forms. Sometimes more than one form is correct.

1 I **was working/would work** in Ontario in 1999 and I **got/used to get** the train at 6.30 every morning.

2 When I was a child you **didn't see/wouldn't see/didn't use to see** much traffic on the roads.

3 My parents **would live/used to live** near a wonderful lake and they **were having/had/would have** two beautiful dogs.

4 In summer, we **were spending/spent/would spend** most of our time outdoors.

5 Sometimes I **used to go/went/would go** on long mountain walks.

C Write the verb in the most likely narrative tense in this magazine article. Sometimes more than one form is correct.

> ### PLANE MAKES EMERGENCY LANDING
>
> Lauren _was_ (1 be) one of 177 passengers. She _____ (2 feel) very excited as she _____ (3 get on) her plane at Gatwick Airport. She _____ (4 wait) a long time for this day - she _____ (5 finally/leave) England to start work in Sofia in Bulgaria two days later.
>
> Lauren was an experienced traveller, and when she was younger she _____ (6 fly) a lot. In those days, her father _____ (7 be) a diplomat and every few years the whole family _____ (8 have to) move to a different country.
>
> Not long after the plane _____ (9 take off) the captain _____ (10 tell) the passengers they _____ (11 have) to return to Gatwick and for the first time Lauren _____ (12 start) to worry. A few minutes later she _____ (13 see) the lights of the airport and _____ (14 wonder) why fire engines and ambulances _____ (15 stand by), but at that time she _____ (16 not know) that the plane's front wheel _____ (17 fall off) during take-off. Suddenly, Lauren _____ (18 feel) an enormous bump, and as the plane _____ (19 come) to a stop some passengers _____ (20 cry). Luckily, the pilot _____ (21 make) a brilliant emergency landing and no-one _____ (22 be injured). Lauren was a little shaken but still confident so she _____ (23 catch) the next flight to Sofia.

D Write sentences about your travel experiences.

1 We were _travelling across the desert_ when _our coach broke down_ .

2 During the school holidays my family would _____ .

3 There were a lot of people in _____ . They were

_____ .

4 When I saw _____ , I _____ .

5 We had _____ but we _____ .

6 I used to _____ but now _____ .

5 My parents, both of whom work, ...

Defining and non-defining relative clauses

Defining relative clauses are necessary for the sense of the sentence.
She is someone **who reads a lot.** (identifies the subject)
That's the car **(that) I sold.** (identifies the object – the relative pronoun can be left out)

Non-defining relative clauses add extra information and are separated by commas.
This book**, which my father gave me,** is very old.

ⓘ We use *which* not *that* for things in non-defining clauses. The relative pronoun cannot be left out.

ⓘ Non-defining relative clauses are more common in written English than spoken English.

ⓘ Relative clauses with prepositions:
Informal: It's a car **(that/which)** I'd pay a lot of money **for.** (preposition at the end)
My brother, **who** I share a flat **with**, is younger than me.
Formal: It's a car **for which** I'd pay a lot of money. (*which* not *that* after prepositions)
My brother, **with whom** I share a flat, is younger than me. (*whom* not *who* after prepositions)
There were a lot of people there, **some/none/many of whom** I'd met before.
Also: *neither/both/some/none/many/the first/the last* + *of* + *whom/which/whose*

A Underline the correct answer.

1 Elephants are the only animals in **Africa that dig/Africa, which dig** deep holes to look for water.

2 The Inuit, **who used/used** to be known as 'Eskimos', live in the coldest parts of the world.

3 According to Mexican legend, November 2nd is the day on **that/which** the dead return to life.

4 The **albatross, which is/albatross that is** a large seabird, can sleep while it flies.

5 Coober Pedy in South Australia is one of the few places in the **world where/world, where** people live underground.

6 The explorer Tristao da Cunha, after **who/whom** the island in the south Atlantic was named, found it impossible to land there.

B Complete the sentences with the correct relative pronoun.

1 The Cambodian language, *which* has 72 letters, has the world's largest alphabet.

2 Maine is the only state in the United States ⎯⎯⎯ name has only one syllable.

3 John Lennon's son, Julian, for ⎯⎯⎯ Paul McCartney wrote the song 'Hey Jude', was born in 1963.

4 There are over 58,000 rocky objects in space, about 900 of ⎯⎯⎯ could crash into the earth.

5 Napoleon Bonaparte is the historical character ⎯⎯⎯ has been portrayed the most in movies – over 190 times!

C Join these pairs of sentences with relative clauses. Add commas where necessary.

1 I bought a book. It was about superstitions.

I bought _a book that/which was about_ superstitions.

2 I got it from a second-hand bookshop. Some of their books are very rare.

I got it _____ are very rare.

3 Superstitions are beliefs about good or bad luck. Many of them are based on old ideas about magic.

Superstitions _____ good or bad luck.

4 Superstitions are largely culture-based. Many books have been written about them.

Superstitions _____ largely culture-based.

5 Actors and sailors have many superstitions. Their occupations are very insecure.

Actors and sailors _____ many superstitions.

6 I know a Japanese girl. She believes that it is bad luck to sleep with your head to the north.

I know _____ with your head to the north.

7 Brazilians have many ancient superstitions. They believe the month of August is unlucky.

Brazilians _____ the month of August is unlucky.

D Expand these sentences using the information in brackets.

1 Diego has two sisters. (neither sister went to university)

Diego has _two sisters, neither of whom went to university_ .

2 Do you know that man? (Maria's talking to him)

Do you know _____ ?

3 In his book *The Motorcycle Diaries*, Che Guevara describes his journey to Peru on a motorbike. (the film's based on the book)

In his book *The Motorcycle Diaries*, _____ .

4 I've got two good friends. (I see both of them regularly)

I've got _____ .

5 I've had many trips to Brazil. (last July was the most recent one)

I've had _____ .

6 He must have known

Certainty about the past			
They	can't/couldn't	have	left.
	must		been working.

Possibility about the past			
She	may/might/could	have	moved.
	may not/might not		been staying there.

ⓘ For questions about possibility we usually use *could*.
Could he **have left**? **Yes,** he **could/might have (done).** (it's possible) **No,** he
can't/couldn't have (done). (certainly not) **Yes,** he **must have (done).** (yes, certainly)
Could she **have been** staying there? **Yes,** she **could/might have been. No,** she
can't/couldn't have been.

A Write the past form of the modal in brackets.

Stonehenge, near Salisbury, England

1 It (must/be) _*must have been*_ a very important religious site.

2 Originally, there (might/be) _____ sixty large stones – many 4 to 7 metres high!

3 'Surely they (can't/move) _____ stones all the way from Wales!' 'Some people think they did.'

4 'How (could/they/make) _____ the stones stand upright?' 'They (must/use) _____ hundreds of men.'

5 '(Could/the Romans/build) _____ it?' 'No, they (could) _____ . It was built about 3100 BC, long before the Romans came to Britain.'

B Look at the pictures and underline the correct answer.

1 The post **must have**/might had/can't have arrived.

2 She **can have/can't have/might have** been on holiday.

3 He **might not have/can't have/must have** forgotten his keys.

4 They **couldn't have/might have/must have** been playing tennis.

5 She **must have slept/can't have slept/might have been sleeping** last night.

C Complete the magazine article. Use one of the modals in brackets in the positive or negative and a verb from the box in the correct form.

be	feel	~~happen~~	have	kill	panic

On 4 December 1872 the *Mary Celeste* was seen floating halfway between the Azores and Portugal. There was no-one on board and the ship was in perfect condition. What (1) _could have happened_ (must/could)? The captain, his wife and two-year-old daughter and the crew of seven were missing and there were no lifeboats. Experts say the crew (2) _____ (may/could) the captain and his family because there was no evidence of a fight. Since the captain and crew left their personal belongings behind, they (3) _____ (must/can) and left in a great hurry. Some people say they (4) _____ (might/can) an accident with the dangerous goods on board and the captain thought the ship was going to explode. Others say they (5) _____ (can/may) a seaquake and the captain tried to get to a nearby island for safety. The truth is no-one knows. Five months later five dead bodies were found on two rafts off the coast of Spain. (6) _____ (Could they/Must they) some of the people on board the *Mary Celeste*?

D Rewrite these sentences using a modal.

1 I'm sure the captain wanted to save his family.
   The captain must have wanted to save his family.

2 Perhaps the bodies weren't the crew of the *Mary Celeste*.
   _____ the crew of the *Mary Celeste*.

3 There definitely wasn't a seaquake – there are no records of one at that time.
   _____ – there are no records of one at that time.

4 Is it possible there was a problem with the goods on board?
   _____ a problem with the goods on board?

5 I'm sure everyone was feeling very frightened.
   _____ very frightened.

6 Is there a chance that it was raining and suddenly there was a storm?
   _____ and suddenly there was a storm?

7 No, no chance – the captain's raincoat was still on board.
   _____ – the captain's raincoat was still on board.

7 It's getting dark

Linking verbs of 'becoming'

	+ adjective/past participle	+ to-infinitive	+ noun	+ prepositional phrase
get	tired/married/dressed	to know		in the way
go	cold/red/deaf/wrong	to sleep		out of fashion
grow	old/bored/dark	to like		
become	famous/anxious/interested		a singer	

ⓘ To express general change *get* is more informal than *become* (*get bigger* = informal)

ⓘ Other linking verbs of 'becoming': *turn (cold, white, nasty), come (to like, to know), fall (ill, asleep, silent), end up (teaching, without any money, in trouble), prove/turn out (to be) (dangerous, useful)*

A Underline the correct answer.

1 I first **got/became** to know Eileen fifty years ago.

2 We **became/grew** to like each other quite quickly.

3 We usually **go/grow** to sleep about 10.00 pm.

4 In the evenings I usually **end up/go** watching television.

5 When I was young I wanted to **come/become** a lawyer.

6 I'm not going to tell you his age - I might **get/become** into trouble!

B Choose the correct linking verb and write it in the gap.

1 When did you ___*get*___ (become/get) married?

2 How did you _____ (come/become) to meet each other?

3 When did you first _____ (go/become) interested in Arthur?

4 Did things ever _____ (go/get) wrong in your early married life?

5 Does he sometimes _____ (go/fall) asleep in front of the television?

6 Do you ever _____ (get/go) bored?

C Write sentences about you.

become	end up	get	prove	go	~~grow~~

1 I don't ___*ever want to grow old!*___ (old)

2 I usually _____ (dressed)

3 I'd _____ (famous)

4 I'd _____ if _____ (crazy)

5 I bought a _____ and _____ (useful)

8 You should have called

ought to/should + have + past participle

I	ought to/should have stayed	on longer at school.	(but I didn't - regret)
You			(but you didn't - criticism)
He	oughtn't to/shouldn't have spent	all the money. (but he did)	

Should(n't)	he	have stayed?	Yes, he **should**	have (done).
			No, he **shouldn't**	
			No, he **needn't** have (done). (not necessary)	

ⓘ *Shouldn't have* is more common than *oughtn't to have*. *Ought to* is rare in questions.

ⓘ We can also use the continuous. He **shouldn't have been** driving so fast. (but he was)

ⓘ We can also use *might* and *could* (in the affirmative only) for regret and criticism.
I **could** have won. (I'm sorry I didn't.) You **might** have told me! (Why didn't you?)

A Write the correct past form of the verbs in brackets.

1 You *should have delivered* (should/deliver) the fridge on Saturday. Why didn't you?

CUSTOMER SERVICES ➡

2 My son _____ (should/not/buy) this game. I want to return it.

3 I'm sorry. We _____ (ought to/call) you back. The television you ordered on the phone is no longer in stock.

4 You _____ (might/tell) me you were closed on Mondays!

5 '_____ (the assistant/should/not/give) me a receipt?' 'Yes, he _____ ?'

6 I _____ (could/get) a much cheaper sofa in the other shop.

B Write sentences in the positive or negative.

1 'I feel sick!' 'You *shouldn't have eaten* so much chocolate.' (eat)

2 We can't get into the concert. All the tickets are sold. We _____ . (book)

3 'You look exhausted.' 'Yes, I _____ to bed earlier last night.' (go)

4 'I haven't got any money!' 'That's your fault! You _____ a new car last week.' (buy)

5 'Chloe's very upset about your comments.' 'She _____ to our conversation!' (listen)

6 This coffee tastes awful. I _____ some sugar in it.' (put)

7 You missed a great party last night. You _____ with us. (come)

9 The man driving the car

Reduced relative clauses

We can reduce some relative clauses to participle clauses:
The boy ~~who is/was~~ **playing** the part of Harry is/was Daniel Radcliffe.
(active - continuous)
The man **living** (= who lives/lived) in the flat comes/came from Chile.
(active - permanent state)
This poster, ~~which was/had been~~ **designed** by a famous artist, won a prize.
(passive - simple)
The houses ~~which are~~ **being built** in the High Street will soon be ready.
(passive - continuous)

A Complete the sentences with one of the verbs in the box in the correct form.

> be considered   call   cost   describe   ~~direct~~   sit   star

1 The film 'Sideways', _directed_ by Alexander Payne, tells the story of two middle-aged friends.
2 The film, _____ Paul Giamatti as Miles, was nominated for an Oscar.
3 Is there an actor _____ Thomas Church in it?
4 I booked two tickets _____ 8 dollars each.
5 The people _____ behind us were talking all the way through the film.
6 When I first heard about the film, George Clooney was the actor _____ for the part of Miles.
7 The film, usually _____ as a comedy, is full of sharp observations about life.

B Rewrite the sentences using a reduced relative clause.

1 I found some old opera records in the attic. They belonged to my mother.
I found some old opera records _belonging to my mother in the attic_ .
2 The records are now worth a lot of money. They were given to her by her father.
The records, _____ .
3 One of the records was my mother's favourite. It was made by Caruso.
One of the records, _____ .
4 Caruso was the eighteenth of twenty-one children. He was born in Naples in 1873.
Caruso, _____ .
5 My mother visited his home in Italy. She was interested in Caruso's life.
My mother, _____ .

10 Every day except Sunday

---

except (for/that/when/where/what etc) (= but not including)

We contacted everyone **except** (**for**) Tom. **Except for** Tom, we contacted everyone.
Everyone **except** (**for**) me (NOT ~~I~~) was sleepy. I walk to work, **except when** it rains. He would have been here earlier, **except** (**that**) he missed the train.
I've done everything **except wash** the car. (*except* + bare infinitive)

besides (= in addition to)

Besides swimm**ing**, I enjoy tennis and golf. (*besides* + noun/-*ing*)

apart from (= but not including/in addition to)

We contacted everyone **apart from** Tom. (= but not including)
Apart from swimming, I enjoy tennis and golf. (= in addition to)
Apart from the fact that he's unqualified, he's not a suitable person for the job.

A A committee is meeting to discuss a conference. Underline the correct answer.

1 We've decided everything <u>**except for**</u>/**besides** a theme for the conference.

2 **Apart from/Except that** Jim Stewart, have you any ideas for a main speaker?

3 **Except/Besides** a morning coffee break, there'll be two afternoon breaks.

4 **Except/Apart from** our main sponsor, who else is supporting the conference?

5 Delegates know everything **except for/besides** where they're staying.

6 I've had positive replies from everyone **apart from/besides** the director. Except for **she/her** they can all come.

7 We've organised everything with the centre except **book/to book** a computer room.

B Rewrite the sentences using *except, besides* and *apart from*.

1 The conference is going well. Unfortunately, not enough people have turned up.
The conference is going well *except that/apart from the fact that not enough people have turned up.*

2 There aren't many staff on duty. There are only a few volunteers.
_____, there aren't many staff on duty.

3 All the speakers have been interesting. However, the main speaker wasn't.
All the speakers have been interesting _____ .

4 The catering is good. But not when the coffee runs out.
The catering is good _____ .

5 There are a lot of other reasons for being here, not only because of the lectures.
_____ there are a lot of other reasons for being here.

Test 1 (Units 1–10)

A Circle the correct answer.

1 The show **had already started/was already starting** when we arrived.

2 Let's **get our photo taken/take our photo** by a professional photographer.

3 Tom's not at home. He **must/can** be on his way.

4 I **would/used to** have long hair but now it's very short.

5 He is someone for **who/whom** I have a lot of respect.

6 She **couldn't have/might not have** forgotten her keys. I saw her pick them up.

7 I didn't say anything because I didn't want to **grow/get** into trouble.

8 You're very late! You **should/must** have got an earlier train.

9 The woman **who hurt/hurt** in the car accident was a friend of mine.

10 I love all food **except for/besides** rice.

[10]

B Write a modal expression to complete the sentences. Use the ideas in brackets.

1 It _____ very pleasant living in that house. (I'm sure it wasn't)

2 He's got a very well-paid job. He _____ very rich. (I'm sure he is)

3 You're very rude! You _____ to her like that. (but you did speak to her like that)

4 It _____ you ages to walk here. It's a long way. (I'm sure it took)

5 I'm working late tonight and I _____ late home for dinner. (it's possible I will be)

6 It _____ a nice day tomorrow. (I expect it will be)

7 She _____ understood your instructions. (it's possible she didn't)

8 They _____ in the library. It's against the rules. (but they were talking)

9 When I was younger I _____ very well. (I was able to sing)

10 You _____ her that I haven't got any money. (I really don't want you to tell her)

[10]

C Complete the sentences with a relative pronoun.

1 I went to see Tim, _____ children I've known since they were young.

2 The new road, about _____ there has been a lot of discussion, will soon be built.

3 She's the woman on _____ we all depend.

4 He's got three cars, all of _____ are brand new.

5 Are you the person _____ phoned this morning?

[5]

D Write the verbs in the correct form.

1 This time yesterday I _____ (have) coffee with my friends.

2 I _____ (be) a supporter of this football club for many years now.

3 When he died, he _____ (make) records for over 30 years.

4 When _____ (you/first/arrive) in this country?

5 All these figures need _____ (check).

6 I _____ (think) of going out tonight. Do you want to come?

7 I _____ (not/meet) him before so I didn't know who he was.

8 I'm having a new kitchen _____ (fit) next week.

9 It _____ (seem) very dark in here. Shall we put on the light?

10 Where are you? It's nearly midday. I _____ (try) to phone you all morning.

	10

E Change two sentences into one. Do not use a relative pronoun.

1 He took no notice of the telephone. It was ringing on his desk.

_____

2 The subject is climate change. It is being discussed at the meeting.

_____

3 A lot of people arrived late. They were invited to the party.

_____

4 The students couldn't see a thing. They were sitting at the back.

_____

5 The man died last night. He had been given an award for bravery.

_____

5

F Correct the mistakes.

1 Sarah has moved house three years ago. _____

2 I must get repaired my laptop. _____

3 He mustn't be driving home; he hasn't got a car. _____

4 We were travelling all day. When we arrived we were hungry. _____

5 She bought two dresses, neither of them was expensive. _____

6 May she have arrived or is it too early? _____

7 Eventually I became to like London. _____

8 You oughtn't to driven so fast. _____

9 Most of the dates were suggested weren't practical. _____

10 Except Brazil, I would like to visit Peru and Mexico. _____

	10

TOTAL

50

11 If I'd seen him, I'd have told him

Third conditional

	If + past perfect,	*would have*	+ past participle
Positive	If it'd (= had) been sunny,	we'd (= would) have	gone sailing.
Negative	If I hadn't gone skiing,	I wouldn't have	broken my leg.
Question	If you'd had the money,	would you have	bought the house?

We use the third conditional for imaginary situations in the past. If it'd been sunny, we'd have gone sailing. (but it wasn't sunny so we didn't go sailing)

ⓘ We can also use:
- other modals to show how possible or sure the result was. If it had been sunny, we could/might have gone sailing.
- the continuous. If I'd been feeling tired, I wouldn't have continued./I wouldn't have been driving if the train had been on time.
- passives. The medicine wouldn't have been discovered if there hadn't been an accident.

A Underline the correct form.

1 If the Titanic **didn't hit**/**hadn't hit** an iceberg, it **wouldn't have sunk**/**doesn't sink**.

2 If the Aztecs **had defeated**/**defeated** Cortes' soldiers, the Spanish **mightn't conquered**/**mightn't have conquered** Mexico.

3 What **happened**/**would have happened** if Columbus **thought**/**had thought** the world was flat?

4 If the Tsar's soldiers **hadn't shot**/**wouldn't shoot** demonstrating workers in 1905, there **mightn't been**/**mightn't have been** a revolution in Russia.

5 John Kennedy **couldn't be assassinated**/**mightn't have been assassinated** in 1963 if he **hadn't been travelling**/**hadn't travelling** in an open-top car.

B Two friends are talking about their old university days. Write the verbs in the correct form.

1 I *'d have gone* (go) to university a year earlier if I'd passed my exams.

2 You _____ (pass) your exams if you'd worked a bit harder.

3 'What _____ (you/study) if you hadn't studied history?' 'I don't know. I _____ (study) politics.'

4 If I _____ (know) the course was going to be so dull, I would have gone somewhere else.

5 If you _____ (not/recommended) that university to me, I _____ (try) to get a place at Cambridge university.

6 If you _____ (go) somewhere else, you _____ (not/meet) your wife!

C Write sentences using the third conditional.

1 As a young child Ellen Macarthur went on a sailing trip with her aunt. A few years later she took up sailing.

If Ellen Macarthur _hadn't gone on a sailing trip_ with her aunt, _she might not have taken up_ sailing.

2 She saved up her school dinner money. She was able to buy a boat.

If she .... money, ... a boat.

3 She decided not to study to be a vet. She became a sailor.

She .... a sailor .... a vet.

4 At 18 she sailed around Britain single-handed. She won the Young Sailor of the Year Award.

She .... the Young Sailor of the Year Award if .... single-handed.

5 She had a good boat. She broke the round-the-world record by 31 hours.

If she .... , she .... by 31 hours.

6 The navigational equipment worked. The boat's generator didn't fail.

If the boat's generator .... , the navigational equipment ....

D Write sentences using the third conditional.

1 I/recognise/you/if/it/not be/dark

I'd have recognised you if it hadn't been dark.

2 If/my alarm/not ring/this morning/I/be/late for work

....

3 If/you/ask/politely/I/lend/you/my car

....

4 If/we/save/more money/we/might/be able to/afford/a holiday abroad

....

5 If/you/read/the instructions/you/not break/the washing machine

....

6 If/you/not remind/me/I/forgot/pay/my tax bill

....

12 Thank you for asking

	verb	(to)	+ object	+ preposition	+ -ing
I'll	**apologise**	to	her	**for**	mak**ing** a mess.
She	**accused**		the man	**of**	driv**ing** badly.
He	**prevented**		the accident	**from**	happen**ing**.
She's	**congratulating**		him	**on**	winn**ing** the race.
He	**forgave**		me	**for**	**not** remember**ing** his birthday.

Other verbs: *admire ... for, advise ... against/about, blame ... for, complain (to ...) about, discourage ... from, excuse ... for, protect ... from, stop ... from, suspect ... of, warn ... against*

A **Complete the letter with a preposition + verb in the correct form.**

Dear Sam,

Excuse me (1) ___*for not writing*___ (not/write) sooner. I've been very busy of late. I want to congratulate you (2) _____ (get) a new job with a hardware company. I don't blame you (3) _____ (want) to move out of that software company you were with. Like you, I would never have been able to forgive them (4) _____ (suspect) you (5) _____ (post) the company's future product plans on the internet. Then they went and accused you (6) _____ (take) money from another software company. Really! I know they apologised to you (7) _____ (make) a mistake but that's not the point. They should have trusted you. I admire you (8) _____ (keep) calm while you proved your innocence. Well done, you!

All the best.

Dominique

B **Join the two sentences with a preposition and the verb in the correct form.**

1 Reisa wants to get a better job. I don't want to discourage her.
I don't want to discourage *Reisa from getting a better job* .

2 The staff shouldn't come in late in the mornings. I've already warned them.
I've already warned _____ .

3 Marina was overworked. She complained to the manager.
Marina complained _____ .

4 You can leave. There's nothing to stop you.
There's nothing to stop _____ .

5 You shouldn't ask your boss for a reference. I strongly recommend you not to.
I strongly advise _____ .

13 The sooner the better

comparative + *and* + comparative
More and more people are shopping on the internet. (emphasising increase)
It's getting **cheaper and cheaper** to travel by plane. (emphasising decrease)

the + comparative + verb + *the* + comparative + verb
The harder we work the happier we are. (one thing affects the other)

the + comparative + *the better*
The bigger the better.

more/not so much + adjective + *than/as* + adjective
It was **more strange than suspicious**. (contrasting two qualities/feelings)
He was **not so much angry as relieved**.

more/less than + adjective/adverb/determiner
I was **less than** happy at the news. (= not very at all)
He was **more than a little** shocked by their rudeness. (= extremely)

A Underline the correct answer in these magazine extracts.

Life in the Twenty First Century

1 People are working **long and long/longer and longer** hours.

2 **The rich/The richer** people get, **the fewer/few** children they choose to have.

3 Are we still looking for cheap holidays? Yes, we are. The cheaper **better/the better**.

4 People are **so much/not so much** healthy as health-conscious.

5 Most of us are less **than/as** enthusiastic about being told to give up our cars.

6 Old people sometimes feel **more confused/confused** than helped by modern technology.

B Complete the sentences.

1 As I get to know Luisa better, I like her more.
The better *I get to know Luisa, the more I like her* .

2 She looks increasingly young each year.
Each year _____ and younger.

3 As she gets older, she gets more attractive.
The older _____ .

4 Her husband Lazlo's not successful at work – he's lazy.
Her husband Lazlo's less _____ – he's lazy.

5 As he works less, he wants to work even less.
The less _____ .

14 We should be told

present modal passive
We **might be asked** to pay. Lasers **can be used** for eye surgery.

perfect modal passive
The door **can't have been locked**. We **should have been told** immediately.

verb + *-ing* passive
I **remember being taught** French. She **likes being taken** out for dinner.
Other verbs + *-ing* passive : *adore, appreciate, fancy, love, not mind*

verb + passive infinitive
I don't **want to be kept** waiting. He will **expect to be met** at the airport.
Other verbs + passive infinitive: *arrange, can't wait, hope, like, 'd love*

get passive (= something happened unexpectedly)
I **got bitten** by a dog. The camera **got broken**. Also: *get + destroyed, killed, lost*

A Complete the sentences with a present modal passive.

1 You must switch off your mobile phones on board the aircraft.
Mobile phones ___*must be switched off*___ on board the aircraft.

2 You should store your luggage in the overhead lockers.
Hand luggage _____ in the overhead lockers.

3 You must switch off portable electronic devices during take off and landing.
Portable electronic devices _____ during take off and landing.

4 You can fill in your landing card on board before arrival.
Landing cards _____ on board before arrival.

B Complete the sentences with *get/got* and a verb from the box in the correct form.

~~damage~~	examine	hurt	lose	stick	take away

1 How did my suitcase _*get damaged*_? It was all right when I checked it in.
2 Make sure you keep the tickets in your handbag so they don't _____ .
3 Be careful opening the lockers. Someone might _____ .
4 We missed our flight so we _____ in Houston overnight.
5 At one airport recently all my luggage _____ and _____ by the police.

C Write the verbs in the correct form and match the two halves of the sentences.

1 Most people believe the Sphinx _must have been built_ (must/build)
2 Some people say it .... (could/create)
3 The building work .... (can't/carry out)
4 The nose .... (might/break off)
5 The face .... (could/wear away)

a .... by an earlier civilisation.
b .... by invading soldiers.
c .... by sand and wind.
d __1__ by Pharoah Khafre.
e .... during the flood season, as was once thought.

D Write the verb in the correct passive form.

1 I remember _being sent_ (send) to Egypt a few years ago by my company.
2 I had arranged .... (meet) at the airport by a taxi.
3 Cairo is such a big city. I didn't fancy .... (lose).
4 I hoped .... (take) round the tourist sites by a specialist guide.
5 I couldn't wait .... (show) the Pyramids.
6 I love .... (look after) when I'm away!

E Write the verbs in the correct passive form in these email extracts.

What's happened to Theo? He (1) _can't have been given_ (can't/give) the sack – he's too good. He (2) .... (must/transfer) to our Athens branch. It's a great place to work – I wouldn't mind (3) .... (offer) a job there.

With a bit of luck we (4) .... (might/give) a big pay rise later this year. It (5) .... (shouldn't/forget) that when the present Government (6) .... (get/elect) they promised big increases for public sector workers. None of us likes (7) .... (undervalue) and people like us always seem (8) .... (get/overlook) by the political parties.

I appreciate (9) .... (ask) to work on your project but recently I (10) .... (get/select) to head up a new research team and I'm tied up for the next few months. Of course I'd love (11) .... (give) the opportunity to work with you later if you still need someone. We (12) .... (should/tell) soon how long the research is to last – in fact we (13) .... (should/tell) already but the Managing Director's away at the moment.

15 There's no need to worry

adjective + *to*-infinitive
We often use adjective + *to*-infinitive:
• to talk about feelings/reactions. I'm **surprised to see** you here.
• for praise or blame. You're **right to leave** now. You're **silly (not) to tell** him.
• to talk about sequence. He was the **first/next/last to arrive**.
• after *it*. **It** was **difficult/easy to understand** him. **It's nice not to have to** go out.

adjective (+ preposition) + *-ing*
He's **busy** study**ing**. This DVD is **worth** watch**ing**. She's **keen on** sail**ing**.
Also: *afraid of, bored with, (no) good at, responsible for, tired of*

noun + *to*-infinitive
This is no **time (for you) to argue**. Also: *decision, desire, need, plan, opportunity*

noun (+ preposition) + *-ing*
What's the **chance of (us) winning**? Also: *difficulty (in), idea of, hope of, problem, thought of*

A Write the verbs in the correct form.

1 I'm relieved ___*to see*___ (see) they're getting married at last.

2 It's not easy _____ (hear) the speech from here. It might be worth _____ (move) a bit closer.

3 'Is there any thought of them _____ (have) children?' 'I think they've made the decision _____ (not/have) any for the time being.'

4 I thought you'd be the last person _____ (get) an invitation!

5 Some of the guests had problems _____ (find) the place.

6 They're very busy. There's no time for them _____ (go) on honeymoon!

B Complete the sentences using the words in brackets.

1 You'll be able to speak to the bride later. (opportunity)
You'll ___*have an opportunity to speak*___ to the bride later.

2 You managed to find a parking space. Was it difficult? (difficulty)
Did you _____ a parking space?

3 Tania refused to come. That wasn't the right thing to do. (wrong)
It was _____ to come.

4 I've been working hard. I've been writing my speech. (busy)
I've been _____ my speech.

5 I can't make speeches. I'm hopeless! (good)
I'm _____ speeches.

16 It's thought to be true

It	+ passive reporting verb	+ that
It	is said/reported	that people are living longer these days.

There	+ passive reporting verb	+ to-infinitive
There	is known/believed	to be/to have been a big problem.

subject	+ passive reporting verb	+ to-infinitive
We	were (not) asked	to	leave.
He	is thought/rumoured		be/have been a fantastic swimmer.

Other verbs: *agree, announce, argue, assume, consider, decide, discover, estimate, expect, fear, feel, find, hope, intend, point out, recommend, show, suggest*

A Write the words in the correct order to complete this newspaper story.

STARS TO SING FOR CHARITY

(1 announced/been/it/has) ___*It has been announced*___ that a huge outdoor charity pop concert is being organised to draw attention to world poverty. At first (2 was/assumed/it) _____ that the whole concert would be televised live but (3 be/thought/to/were/there) _____ problems with this idea. (4 be/said/our leading charities/to/are) _____ delighted with this initiative and even the Government (5 welcomed/believed/is/to/have) _____ the news. However, when (6 give/were/the public/to/asked) _____ their opinion, most were doubtful. While (7 been/shown/it/has) _____ that such concerts raise public awareness, they say the Government will never do anything to solve the problem. Only major changes to the way our taxes are spent would make a difference and (8 expected/this/not/happen/is/to) _____ .

B Complete the second sentence so that it has a similar meaning to the first. Do not use *by*.

1 The organisers hope that the world's most famous artists will appear.
It *is hoped that* _____ the world's most famous artists will appear.

2 Some people fear that bad weather might spoil the concert.
It _____ bad weather might spoil the concert.

3 Some people have suggested that the President should make a speech.
It _____ the President should make a speech.

4 The organisers expect that over 100,000 people will attend.
It _____ over 100,000 people will attend.

C Rewrite the sentences.

1 It was said that Cleopatra was the most beautiful woman in the world.
Cleopatra *was said to be/to have been* the most beautiful woman in the world.

2 It is thought that the Ancient Romans were the first to wear engagement rings.
The Ancient Romans _____ the first to wear engagement rings.

3 It was rumoured that Sigmund Freud failed as a hypnotist.
Sigmund Freud _____ as a hypnotist.

4 It is believed that King Henry VIII of England was a keen football player.
King Henry VIII of England _____ a keen football player.

5 It is reported that the ghost of his fourth wife still haunts Hampton Court Palace.
The ghost of his fourth wife _____ Hampton Court Palace still.

6 It is considered that Alexander the Great was the greatest military general ever.
Alexander the Great _____ the greatest military general ever.

D Expand the news headlines in two different ways, using the verbs in brackets.

1 **THREE SUSPECTS IN LATEST BANK ROBBERY** (think)
There *are thought to be three suspects* in the latest bank robbery.
It *is thought that there are three suspects* in the latest bank robbery.

2 **20,000 REFUGEES IN FAMINE CRISIS** (estimate)
There _____ in the famine crisis.
It _____ in the famine crisis.

3 **SOFTWARE COMPANY MAKING BIGGER PROFITS** (report)
It _____ bigger profits.
The software company _____ bigger profits.

4 **KILLER HAS COMMITTED OVER 100 CRIMES** (know)
The killer _____ over 100 crimes.
It _____ over 100 crimes.

5 **BIG EARTHQUAKE IN SOUTHERN EUROPE** (believe)
There _____ in southern Europe.
It _____ in southern Europe.

17 Had I realised, I ...

Conditionals and alternatives to *if*

We use zero and first conditionals for **real** situations.
If you **lose** your card, the bank **gives/will give** you a new one. (possible future situation)
If it **was raining**, we **used to** stay indoors. (regular, true event in the past)

We use second and third conditionals for **unreal** situations.
If you **met** the Queen, what **would** you **say**? (unlikely/hypothetical situation in the future)
If you**'d listened**, you**'d have understood**. (but you didn't listen – past situation)

ⓘ We can use the following alternatives to *if*:

What if		fails?		will		(real situation)
Suppose	your plan		What		you do then?	
Supposing		failed?		would		(unlikely)

Take my phone number **in case** (= because of the possibility) you need to phone me.
You **won't get** there on time **unless** the taxi **arrives** soon. (prediction/warning)
Let's hope the weather improves. **Otherwise** (= If it doesn't), we'll have to stay at home.

ⓘ We can use the following formal alternatives to *if*:
were + subject + *to*-infinitive: **Were we to offer** you the job, would you take it?
should + subject + verb: **Should you find** yourself in Paris, give us a ring.
had + subject + past participle: **Had you listened**, you would have understood.
But for (= If it hadn't been for) your help, we would have failed.

A Underline the correct answer.

1 If the fight **lasts/<u>had lasted</u>** longer, I**'d enjoy/
<u>'d have enjoyed</u>** it more.

2 Ercan **won/would have won** if he **hadn't been/
wasn't** injured.

3 If Jozsef **wins/will win** again next month, he**'ll/'d**
be world champion.

4 If there **are/were** any tickets left for tonight's fight,
do/will you get me one?

5 I**'ll/'d feel** happier if Ercan still **had/had had** his old trainer with him.

B Complete the sentences with *were*, *had* or *should*.

1 *Had* he taken part in the fight, he would have won!

2 .... he ever need an agent, let me know.

3 .... he retired last year, it would have been a big mistake.

4 .... he to want another sponsor, I know a company that would be interested.

5 .... he call me, I'll ask him to get in touch with you.

C Write the verbs in the correct form.

1 (Muhammad Ali/box) _Were Muhammad Ali to box_ today, (the sport/be) _the sport would be_ a lot more exciting.

2 If (he/not/begin) _____ boxing so young, (he/not/become) _____ such a good boxer.

3 (He/get) _____ hurt a lot more than he did if (he/not/be) _____ so fast on his feet.

4 Even today, if (there/be) _____ a discussion about boxing, (people/still/say) _____ he was the greatest.

5 (He/not/be) _____ sentenced to prison in 1967 if (he/not/refuse) _____ to join the army.

D Rewrite the sentences using the word in brackets. Make any necessary changes.

1 If you don't train hard, you won't win an Olympic medal. (unless)
You _won't win an Olympic medal unless you_ train hard.

2 Kelly Holmes wouldn't have won two gold medals if it hadn't been for her dedication. (but for)
_____ two gold medals.

3 Imagine me going in for the marathon. Do you think I could win? (what if)
_____ ? Do you think I could win?

4 Would Cathy Freeman beat me if she were running today? (suppose)
_____ beat me?

5 If you love the sport, you'll do well. (provided that)
You _____ the sport.

6 Paula Radcliffe would have finished the race if she hadn't felt unwell. (otherwise)
Paula Radcliffe _____ the race.

E Write the verbs in the most likely form.

'I didn't play very well this afternoon. I _'d have done_ (1 do) better if I _____ (2 have) a good night's sleep last night. Sometimes I get fed up with sport. The truth is that unless it _____ (3 be) an important game, I _____ (4 find) it difficult to motivate myself. I know that if I _____ (5 keep) in shape more, I _____ (6 be) a lot more successful than I am but I enjoy my social life too much. In fact, if I _____ (7 practise) every day when I was younger instead of going out with my friends, I _____ (8 win) some major competitions.'

18 However, it was very late

in spite of/despite	
I couldn't sleep **despite/in spite of**	feel**ing** tired. (+ *-ing*)
	my **tiredness**. (+ noun)
	the fact that I was tired. (+ *the fact that*)

although/(even) though/however/nevertheless

I went out **although/(even) though** it was very cold. (linking parts of a sentence)
It was cold. **However,/Nevertheless,/Even so,** I went out. (linking across sentences)

while/whereas (= comparing difference)

Some students work very hard **while/whereas** others are very lazy.

A Write the correct word in the gaps.

1 ___*Although*___ I don't usually like art exhibitions, this one looks good. (however/although)

2 I like a good jazz concert _____ Marco prefers to go to the cinema. (while/nevertheless)

3 I tried to get seats for the opera. _____ , the tickets were sold out. (Even though/However)

4 I really enjoyed the Glastonbury Festival last year _____ the crowds. (whereas/in spite of)

5 It took us hours to get to the theatre. _____ , it was well worth it. (Even so/Even though)

> **What's On Guide**
>
> Art
> Jazz
> Theatre   Festivals
> Concerts   Opera

B Rewrite the sentences using the word in brackets.

1 Although Joseph Conrad wrote all his novels in English, his first language was Polish. (however)
Joseph Conrad wrote all his novels in English. However, his first language was Polish.

2 Despite the fact that his guardian wanted him to follow a different career, he was determined to go to sea. (although)
_____ , he was determined to go to sea.

3 He was only 17. Even so, he joined a ship and crossed the Atlantic. (in spite of)
_____ a French ship and crossed the Atlantic.

4 Although many novelists wrote about domestic dramas, Conrad wrote about the sea. (whereas)
Many novelists _____ the sea.

5 Even though famous writers praised his novels, at first they weren't very popular. (nevertheless)
_____ very popular.

	(auxiliary)	focus adverb	adjective/noun/verb
He	's (not)	**even**	written a letter! (it's very surprising)
She	couldn't		remember my name!
His work	is	**simply/just**	terrible. (I feel strongly about it)
It	was	**simply/just/only**	a joke. (nothing else – it's not important)
We			need a bit more time. (nothing more)

Focus adverbs emphasise the most important part of what we are talking about.
I'm (not) **particularly/especially** interested in going there. (more than usual)
It's rained a lot recently, but it was a(n) **particularly/especially** wet day yesterday.
We **mainly/mostly** listen to jazz. (usually)
He doesn't do much sport, **mainly/mostly because** he's too busy. (the main reason)

ⓘ *Only, just, simply* and *even* can begin a sentence. **Only** three people knew the answer.
Just/Simply write your name here. **Even** Tom likes jazz.

ⓘ I like walking, **even if/even when** it's raining.

A Write the correct word in the gaps.

FAMOUS QUOTATIONS

1 "I pay no attention to anybody's praise or blame. I _simply_ follow my own feelings." Mozart (*even/simply*)

2 "Age is not a _____ interesting subject. Anyone can get old. All you have to do is live long enough." Groucho Marx (*just/particularly*)

3 "Politicians are all the same. They promise to build a bridge _____ when there's no river." Nikita Khrushchev (*simply/even*)

4 "Comedy is _____ a funny way of being serious." Peter Ustinov (*simply/even*)

5 "I'm _____ going outside and may be some time." Captain Oates' last words (*mostly/just*)

6 "Don't walk behind me; I may not lead. Don't walk in front of me; I may not follow. _____ walk beside me and be my friend." Albert Camus (*Especially/ Just*)

B Rewrite the sentences, using the adverbs in brackets.

1 I understood the film. No-one else did. (only)
 Only I understood the film . No-one else did.

2 He couldn't take the time to phone me. He's so rude. (even)
 _____ . He's so rude.

3 I eat toast for breakfast. That's all. (only)
 _____ . That's all.

4 We don't go out very often, because we haven't got much money. (mainly)
 _____ much money.

20 Swimming is my favourite sport

-ing as subject	
(Your) travelling by train **Not getting any exercise**	**makes** me nervous. (in general) **is** very bad for your health.

Question word as subject	
What he's saying **Whoever said that**	**doesn't make** any sense. **is** mad.

That clause as subject	
That he looked so old	**came** as something of a shock.

To-infinitive as subject	
(Not) to go with you	never **crossed** my mind.

ⓘ *That* and the *to*-infinitive are less common as subjects in informal English. We normally say: **It** (came as something of a shock) **that** … **It** (never crossed my mind) **to** …

A Underline the correct alternative.

1 Achieving/<u>What you've achieved</u> is very impressive.

2 **That you start/Starting** your own business requires a lot of effort.

3 **That you survived/Not surviving** is quite amazing.

4 **How much more we should spend/To spend** is something we're thinking about.

5 **What we borrowed/Borrowing money** is very expensive.

6 **That we expand/Not to have expanded** would have been a mistake.

B Rewrite the sentences without using *it*.

1 It depends on the market how fast we expand.
   How fast we expand depends on the market.

2 It's wrong to compare what we do with our competitors.
   .... with our competitors ....

3 It takes time finding the right staff.
   .... time.

4 It's our aim to expand overseas.
   .... our aim.

5 It's always possible that we might fail.
   .... possible.

6 It's a secret what our next product is going to be.
   .... secret.

Test 2 (Units 11–20)

A Circle the correct answer.

1 I wouldn't have overslept if I **set/had set** the alarm.
2 He apologised **for being/to be** late.
3 The **old/older** I get the **happy/happier** I am.
4 That film should **ban/be banned**!
5 She's always the last **to leave/leave**.
6 They are said **being/to be** millionaires.
7 **Should/Were** you need any help, just let me know.
8 I only had a sandwich, **whereas/even so** you had a big lunch.
9 There aren't any fish in the river, **even/mostly** because of pollution.
10 **What/That** I need is something to drink.

10

B Write the verbs in the correct form.

1 If you _____ (go) to the show last night, you _____ (enjoy) it.
2 He _____ (might/cure) last week if the doctor _____ (call) sooner.
3 I don't want to discourage you from _____ (apply) for the job.
4 Why did she get _____ (arrest)?
5 I remember _____ (tell) stories as a child by my father.
6 It's easy _____ (see) why he's so successful.
7 It _____ (announce) last night that the President will travel to Bulgaria.
8 _____ (I/know) there was going to be a strike, I wouldn't have gone.
9 What if the plane _____ (delay)? What shall we do?
10 _____ (learn) a new language is never easy.

10

C Write the words in the correct order.

1 (for/me/asking/forgive) _____ but how old are you?
2 (food/more/enough/than/there's) _____ for everyone. Look!
3 (no/there's/worry/need/you/to/for) _____ . Everything's organised.
4 (student/particularly/clever/a/she's) _____ . She always gets A grades.
5 (yourself/help/just) _____ . It's all free.

5

35

D Write one word in each gap.

1 I don't blame you .... not telling her the real reason.

2 Congratulations .... passing your driving test!

3 He's not .... much unfit .... lazy.

4 This town is getting quieter .... quieter.

5 He can't have .... given the key, surely! He's too irresponsible.

6 There's absolutely no hope .... ever finding the ring. It's lost forever.

7 .... you to go by train, you'd save a lot of money.

8 .... I try hard to play the guitar, I don't seem to be improving.

9 He didn't .... know where the post office was. How strange!

10 .... you know the truth. No-one else.

10

E Change the two sentences into one. Use the words in brackets.

1 We didn't catch the train. We were looking for a taxi for half the night. (if)

....

2 The weather was bad. I still enjoyed myself. (despite)

....

3 He's got a good job. However, he still complains. (even though)

....

4 I didn't enjoy the evening. He was rude. (but for)

....

5 People learn in different ways. That's not a new idea. (that people)

....

5

F Correct the mistakes.

1 If you <u>would have taken</u> the test, you would have passed ....

2 I couldn't stop the child <u>to cry</u>. ....

3 The more <u>it is expensive</u>, the better the food generally. ....

4 You can't expect <u>that you are put</u> in the same class. ....

5 I'm surprised <u>hearing</u> that he's put on weight. ....

6 It <u>hoped</u> that they'll find the papers soon. ....

7 You won't find any shops open unless you <u>don't get</u> a move on ....

8 They didn't earn much money in spite of <u>they worked</u> very hard. ....

9 <u>Especially I'm not keen</u> on opera. ....

10 Whoever <u>did I speak</u> to was very polite. ....

10

TOTAL

50

21 I wish I'd known

wish	+ past perfect simple/continuous (to express regret about a past situation)
I wish	we'd (had) taken your advice. (but we didn't)
	I hadn't refused the job offer. (but I did)
	I could have been there. (but I wasn't) NOT ~~I wish I would have been~~ ...
He **wishes**	he hadn't been sitting in the sun all day. (but he was)
ⓘ *If only* expresses a stronger regret. **If only** we'd taken your advice!	

A Some football players are talking after a match. Write the verbs in the correct form.

1 I wish their goalkeeper _hadn't saved_ (not/save) that penalty.

2 If only we _____ (play) the whole game more positively!

3 I wish you _____ (pass) the ball to Ronaldo.

4 When they got the ball, I wish I _____ (not/lie) on the ground injured.

5 I wish we _____ (have) a full team with no injuries.

6 If only the referee _____ (not/stop) the game!

B Underline the correct answer.

1 I feel awful. If only I **hadn't eaten**/**didn't eat** that shellfish last night!

2 What a great view! I wish we **brought**/**'d brought** our camera.

3 I'm so tired. I wish I**'d had**/**had** more energy.

4 I missed the best part of the show. If only I **had**/**hadn't** left so early!

5 If only I **wasn't driving**/**hadn't been driving** so fast when the police saw me!

6 Keep quiet you two! I wish you **would read**/**had read** a book or do your homework!

C Complete the sentences for you in the past or the present/future. Use the positive or negative.

1 I wish I _hadn't bought an expensive coat last week_ . (buy)

2 I wish I _____ . (remember)

3 If only I _____ ! (have)

4 I wish I _____ . (can)

5 I wish I _____ . (learn)

22 On account of the rain

because of/on account of/owing to/due to/as a result of + noun (to give reason)		
The train was delayed	**because of/owing to/due to on account of/as a result of**	**the bad weather**.

ⓘ We can also say: The event was cancelled **because of/on account of/owing to/due to/in view of** + **the fact that** not many tickets were sold.

because/as/since/seeing as/seeing that/given that + subject + verb		
I can't come to the meeting next week	**because/as/since/seeing as/ seeing that/given that**	**I'm** on holiday.
Seeing as/that **Given that/Since/As**	it's your money, you can do what you like.	

so/therefore/as a result/consequently/that's why + subject + verb (to give result)		
The company was doing badly,	**so**	
The company was doing badly	**and** **so/therefore/as a result/consequently/ that's why**	**it closed**.
The company was doing badly.	**Therefore,/As a result,/ Consequently,/That's why**	

A Underline the correct answer.

1 I felt stressed **as/because of** I'd been overworking recently.

2 I wanted to learn to relax. **That's why/Seeing that** I went to a hypnotist.

3 Hiroshi went to an acupuncturist **because/because of** his bad back.

4 Sonia had bad stomach pains and **since/therefore** I recommended a herbal remedy.

5 **Due to/Consequently** the teacher's good reputation, the yoga classes were always crowded.

6 **In view of/As** the fact that homeopathy can be very effective for some illnesses, it is becoming increasingly popular.

7 **Seeing as/As a result** we lead such pressurised lives these days, it's not surprising we need help.

B Match the two parts of the sentence.

1 I can't get out of this chair because of _c_   **a** an hour ago I couldn't move.

2 I've just had a great yoga massage and as a result ....   **b** the massage.

3 I love a head massage as ....   **c** a bad pain in my back.

4 My headache's disappeared due to ....   **d** I feel very relaxed.

5 It's amazing that I can walk given that ....   **e** it always relaxes my muscles.

C Complete the sentences using the words in brackets.

1 I had to go on a diet because I was putting on weight.
I was putting on weight. Therefore I had to go
(or ... _weight and therefore_ ...) on a diet. (therefore)

2 It's important to be healthy. That's why you should get plenty of sleep. (since)

....
important to be healthy.

3 Junk food is full of fat, so you shouldn't eat too much of it. (seeing)

.... of fat.

4 As Susie was stressed, the doctor told her to take regular exercise. (account)

.... her stress.

5 There was more fruit in Tom's diet. Consequently, his health improved. (because)

.... in his diet.

6 My mother took up a hobby because she wanted to keep her brain active. (therefore)

.... took up a hobby.

D Use the expressions from the box to link the two sentences. You may make one or two sentences. There is more than one possible answer.

as	as a result	consequently	due to the fact that	that's why	therefore

1 I was depressed. I went out and booked a weekend away.
As I was depressed, I went out and booked a weekend away. or
I was depressed. As a result, I went out and booked a weekend away.

2 I had to stay in a cheap hotel. I didn't have much money.

....

3 It was raining. I couldn't go for long walks.

....

4 I was bored. I decided to get a taxi and go window shopping.

....

5 The town was very lively. There was a street festival going on.

....

6 Everyone was very friendly. I made lots of friends.

....

23 She's famous for singing

	adjective	+ preposition	(+ object)	+ -ing
I'm	**sorry**	**for/about**		interrupt**ing**.
	frightened	**of**	**him**	hurt**ing** himself.
	disappointed	**at/about**		**not** gett**ing** the job.

Also: *responsible for, concerned about, amazed at, capable of, angry at*

	noun	+ preposition	(+ object)	+ -ing
There's no	**point**	**in**	**(him)**	worry**ing**.

Also: *effect of, delay in, chance of, means of, apology for, hope of, insistence on*

	adjective	(+ *that*)	+ clause
I'm	**sorry**	**(that)**	I interrupted.
	frightened		you might hurt yourself.

A Complete the sentences using a preposition + -ing.

1 Is there any chance that we will ever increase our circulation?
Is there any chance _of us ever increasing_ our circulation?

2 The owner is concerned that we will lose money.
The owner is concerned .... money.

3 I'm frightened that he will close down the newspaper.
I'm frightened .... down the newspaper.

4 His insistence that journalists work longer hours is very demotivating.
His insistence .... longer hours is very demotivating.

5 Do you think there's any hope that things will get better?
Do you think there's any hope .... better?

B Complete this email from the newspaper owner to the journalists with a preposition and the verb in the correct form.

I'm sorry about the delay (1) _in communicating_ (communicate) to you all but I've been away. When I returned from my holiday I was very angry (2) .... (hear) that our sales figures had dropped so badly. Consequently, the Editor, who is responsible (3) .... (make sure) that people want to read the paper, has been asked to leave and a new Editor has been appointed.

As a means (4) .... (increase) sales the new Editor and I have decided to concentrate a lot more on stories about celebrities. I'm disappointed (5) .... (have to) cut down on more serious news stories but if we are not capable (6) .... (write) serious stories that interest people then we have to make changes. The effect (7) .... (not do) so would be disastrous for sales and I make no apology (8) .... (make) our stories less serious if necessary.

24 I'll be waiting for you

will/won't be + -ing (future continuous)

Positive: I**'ll be** com**ing** to the meeting tonight.
Negative: They **won't be** leav**ing** until tomorrow.
Question: **Will** you **be** com**ing** to the meeting tonight?

ⓘ We can also say: **I'm going to/may/might/should be** get**ting** a new job soon.

We use the future continuous:
- to talk about a temporary activity that is going on at a certain time in the future. I**'ll be** watch**ing** the tennis match this afternoon.
- to talk about a future event that has already been arranged. We**'ll be** mov**ing** to Germany in July.
- to talk about something that will happen as part of a routine. I**'ll be** see**ing** my mother on Friday as usual.
- to ask politely about people's intentions. **Will** you **be** us**ing** the car later on?
- to predict something that is happening now. Don't go in! They**'ll be** hav**ing** lunch.

ⓘ We do not usually use the future continuous with state verbs (*be, know, love* etc).

A Complete the sentences with a verb from the box in the future continuous.

go	need	see	~~sit~~	think	work

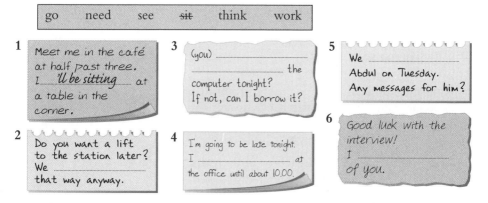

1 Meet me in the café at half past three. I *'ll be sitting* at a table in the corner.

2 Do you want a lift to the station later? We .... that way anyway.

3 (you) .... the computer tonight? If not, can I borrow it?

4 I'm going to be late tonight. I .... at the office until about 10.00.

5 We .... Abdul on Tuesday. Any messages for him?

6 Good luck with the interview! I .... of you.

B Underline the correct answer.

1 <u>Will you be getting up</u>/Do you get up early tomorrow? If so, can you wake me?

2 Pay me the money. Then I**'ll send/'ll be sending** you the CD.

3 Don't phone Sarah. She**'ll have/'ll be having** her hair done at the moment.

4 Put the heating on. We**'re going to be coming/come** back home this evening.

5 Your guide **should wait/should be waiting/is waiting** for you at the airport when you arrive.

6 **Will you go/Will you be going** anywhere near the post office later? If so, can you buy me a stamp?

C Write the verbs in the future continuous or *will* (simple future).

1 ' *Will you be going* (you/go) to the meeting tonight? If so,
we *'ll give* (give) you a lift.'
'Thanks, but I don't think I .... (be) home in time.'

2 'I need more information about the project. ....
(you/email) it to me?'
'Sure. .... (you/work) on it tomorrow? If so, I
.... (send) you the stuff tonight.'

3 'Tell me. What .... (you/do) at 10.00 tonight?'
'I .... (probably/get) ready for bed. Why?'

4 'Put your seat belt on. The plane .... (take off) in a few minutes.'
'Take it easy. I .... (put) it on when the light comes on. Not
before.'

5 'I .... (not/stay) here much longer. I've got a job in Canada.'
'Lucky you. I .... (come) and visit you there next summer!'

6 '................................ (you/use) your car tonight? If not, can I borrow it?
'OK, but you .... (have to) bring it back tomorrow morning. I
need it for work.'

D Write the verbs in the future continuous or *will* (simple future).

1 Interviewer: What do you think you *'ll be doing* (do) in five years' time?

2 Carlos: In five years' time I .... (be) 26 years old and I hope I
.... (earn) lots of money.

3 Rosa: I'm sure I .... (live) abroad and I .... (have) a
good job with a big multinational company.

4 Roberta: In five years' time I .... (take) my final exams at university
and I .... (still/live) at home.

5 Juan: I .... (be) retired in five years' time and I ....
(spend) my time reading and listening to music.

E Write sentences saying what you will be doing in five years' time.

1 I think I ....

2 I might ....

3 I hope I ....

4 I'm sure I ....

5 I don't think I ....

25 The book came out last year

Phrasal verbs which do not take an object (intransitive): verb + particle

The missing computer eventually **turned up.**
Also: *take off* (succeed), *pass away* (die), *grow up, come out* (be published)

Phrasal verbs which take an object (transitive): verb + particle + object

He **looked up the information** on the internet.
Can you **look after the business** while I'm away?
Also: *put on* (perform), *set up* (establish), *look into* (investigate), *bring up* (care for a child until they are an adult), *cut off* (separate), *think of* (consider)

Phrasal verbs with two particles: verb + particle + preposition

Ian really **looks up to** his brother. (respect)
Also: *get on with, put up with* (tolerate), *look forward to*

Phrasal verbs in the passive: *be* + past participle + particle

Make sure the lights **are switched off** before you leave.

ⓘSome verbs are more commonly used in the passive. We **were cut off** from the others.
Also: *be caught up in, be handed down, be sworn in, be thought of*

A Complete the biography with phrasal verbs in the correct form.

Derek Walcott, poet and playwright (b.1930)

Derek Walcott, the Nobel prize-winning poet and playwright, (1) ___*grew up*___ on the Caribbean island of St Lucia, an ex-British colony. He was only a few years old when his father, a painter, (2) _____ and he (3) _____ by his mother, who ran the island's Methodist school. Walcott's first book of poems (4) _____ when he was only 18, and in 1959 he (5) _____ the Theatre Workshop in Trinidad, which subsequently (6) _____ many of his plays. However, his career didn't really (7) _____ until the collection of poems 'In a Green Night' in 1962. Today, throughout the world, Walcott (8) _____ as one of the finest poets of recent years and in the Caribbean he is seen as a role model for other artists to (9) _____ , but he himself sometimes feels he (10) _____ from the common life of poorer Caribbean people as a result of his colonial heritage. In his poems and plays, Walcott (11) _____ the confusions of this complex heritage and explores his cultural identity with considerable skill and sophistication.

B Write the verbs in the passive using the tense in brackets.

1 I ___*was brought up*___ (bring up) on an island in the Caribbean. (past simple)

2 My plays _____ (put on) around the world. (present perfect)

3 A new theatre _____ (set up) on another one of the islands. (*will* future)

4 We _____ (cut off) from many outside influences. (past simple)

5 I _____ (think of) as more of a poet than a dramatist. (present simple)

26 He promised to tell her

verb + (not) to-infinitive	verb + object + (not) to-infinitive
He **promised to visit** her. I **threatened not to pay** the bill. Also: *agree, ask, offer, promise, refuse, threaten*	I **advised her to sit down.** Also: *advise, ask, encourage, invite, order, persuade, remind, tell, urge*

verb + object + preposition + -ing	verb + preposition (+ object) + -ing
They **criticised him for** doing the job so badly. Also: *blame, criticise, praise*	She **insisted on** (**me**) stay**ing** for lunch. Also: *apologise for*

verb + object + that	verb (+ preposition + object) + that
He **persuaded me that** I should come. Also: *advise, convince, promise, remind, tell*	He **complained** (**to me**) **that** there was no-one there. Also: *agree, admit, argue, explain, insist, mention, say, suggest*

verb + (not) -ing
She **reported** hearing/hav**ing heard** a noise. Also: *admit, deny, mention, regret* They **suggested** hav**ing** lunch. Also: *propose, recommend*

A Two colleagues are talking about a client. Write the correct verb.

1 They __denied__ having visited other companies. (promised/denied)

2 Sophie _____ them that we were the right organisation. (convinced/explained)

3 Did you _____ to them that we have an office in Japan? (advise/mention)

4 We _____ them to look round the laboratory. (persuaded/proposed)

5 Their managing director _____ to offer us a better price. (refused/suggested)

6 They _____ not bringing their accountant. (agreed/regretted)

7 They _____ for not making a decision today. (apologised/threatened)

B A manager is talking about yesterday's meeting. Write the words in brackets in the correct form and add a preposition where necessary. There may be more than one possible answer.

1 Mark _promised to contact_ (promise/contact) the bank in the morning.

2 Tania _____ (suggest/take) the client out for a meal.

3 The Finance Director _____ (advise/us/forget) the deal.

4 I _____ (remind/Tania/not/forget) to phone the company again.

5 The Chief Executive _____ (admit/be) disappointed with the latest offer.

6 He _____ (insist/we/negotiate) a better contract.

C Make sentences from these words in the correct form and any other words you need. There may be more than one possible answer.

1 Ben/convince/me/he/able to/repair/my laptop
Ben convinced me that he was able to repair my laptop.

2 He/admit/damage/the hard disk

3 He/explain/me/he/not really understand/the problem

4 He/apologise/me/ruin/the machine

5 He/offer/lend/me/his laptop

6 I/suggest/he/buy/me/a new one

7 I/remind/him/I/lose/a lot of data

8 I/not invite/him/stay/with me again!

D Report the direct speech using one of the verbs from the box. You will need to leave out or change words.

agree	complain	encourage	insist	~~threaten~~

1 'I'm going to take you to court!'
He threatened to take me to court.

2 'You're always playing your music so loudly!'

3 'No, please, let me pay. I want to.'

4 'You should really try for a place at university. I think you've got a really good chance of getting in.'

5 'OK, let's not talk about it again.'

27 Turn it on

Separable and inseparable phrasal verbs

With separable phrasal verbs the object can come before or after the particle.
Can you **drop Tom off** at school? Can you **drop off Tom** at school?
Also: *add in, bring back, clear up, cut up, fill in/up, give back, heat up, keep down, let out, make up, put down, stir in, switch on, take off, throw away, try on, write down*

ⓘ If the object is a long phrase it must come after the particle. Could you **fill in the form on the table**? NOT ~~Could you fill the form on the table in?~~

ⓘ If the object is a pronoun it must come before the particle. Could you **fill it in**, please? NOT ~~Could you fill in it?~~

With inseparable phrasal verbs the object always comes after the particle. She **looked for her bag**. NOT ~~She looked her bag for.~~ Also: *come from, get at, laugh at, take after, cut down on, put up with, run out of*

ⓘ Intransitive phrasal verbs do not have an object. My car **broke down** yesterday.
Also: *boil over, come on, get by, go off, stand up*

A Underline the correct answers in this recipe extract.

1 **Cut up the beetroot/Cut the beetroot up** into small pieces.

2 **Add in the chopped celery, red pepper, onion and carrot./ Add the chopped celery, red pepper, onion and carrot in.**

3 Take the saucepan and **fill it up/fill up it** with water.

4 **Stir in the cumin seeds./Stir the cumin seeds in.**

5 **Heat up the stove./Heat the stove up.**

6 Make sure the soup doesn't **boil over/boil it over**.

7 To **cut down on calories/cut calories down on** use fat-free sour cream when serving.

Borscht

B Complete the sentence using one of the verbs in the box. If possible, separate the verb and the particle.

| clear up | go off | ~~make up~~ | run out of |
| take off | throw away | | |

1 I can't find the recipe so I'll have to _____make it up_____ . (invent it)

2 If the cream _____ , don't use it. (no longer fresh)

3 If you _____ , use black caviar. (haven't got any more red caviar left)

4 When you've boiled the tomatoes, _____ . (remove the skins)

5 When you've done that, _____ . (discard them)

6 _____ when you've finished. (tidy the kitchen)

28 She will have left

A Write the verbs in the future perfect.

1 Before the next election the number of people receiving free bus travel
   will have risen (rise) by 9%.

2 By the end of the financial year the company _____ (sell) over
   twelve million computers, significantly boosting its profits.

3 When it is finally completed the new Olympic Stadium _____
   (cost) over £750 million.

4 If the newspaper relocates its offices outside the capital, it _____
   (create) many new jobs by the end of the year.

5 A new government bill is being debated in Parliament tomorrow, but politicians
   are complaining that they _____ (not/have) a chance to read it by
   then.

6 One union leader asked 'What _____ (change) in my members'
   lives by this time next week? The answer is they'll be poorer.'

B Complete a politician's promises using the idea in brackets and the future perfect.

By the time we've been in power for five years …

1 _____ *… we will have built more hospitals.* _____ (health)
2 _____ (education)
3 _____ (crime)
4 _____ (what people earn)
5 _____ (transport)

C A politician's secretary is trying to arrange appointments. Complete the sentences using *will* (simple future), future continuous or future perfect.

1 'Can I arrange a meeting for 8.45?'

'I'm sorry. She *'ll be having* (have) breakfast with the Press Secretary at that time.'

2 'I must speak to her before she meets the Prime Minister. Can I meet her at 10.00?'

'Too late, I'm afraid. She .... (met) the Prime Minister by then.'

Wednesday	
8.30	Breakfast with the Press Secretary
9.30	Meeting with the Prime Minister
10.00	Press conference
11.00	Greet a foreign delegation
12.00	Lunch
14.00	Free
15.00	Drive to the airport
17.00	Fly to New York

3 'OK then. I .... (see) her at 11.15, if that's OK.'

'Sorry. She .... (talk) to a foreign delegation at that time.'

4 'Don't let her talk to the press until I get there at 12.00.'

'Can't you get here earlier? The press conference .... (finish) by that time.'

5 'I'd like to take her out for lunch, say at 1.00.'

'No. She .... (already/have) lunch by then and she .... (not/be) free until 2.00.'

6 'I'd like her to meet an important client just after 3.00.'

'Unfortunately she .... (drive) to the airport at that time.'

7 'I've got an idea. I'll meet her at the airport at 5.30.'

'No, she .... (already/leave) for New York by then.'

D Make predictions for the year 2100. Use the verbs in the box in the future perfect with *will/won't/might/may/should* in the active or passive.

eradicate	find	land	ruin	run out	~~take over~~

1 The internet *might have taken over* the work of teachers.

2 The world's oil ....

3 Hunger .... from the poorest countries.

4 Climate change .... many parts of the world.

5 A cure .... for cancer.

6 Men .... on Mars.

29 I'll have been working here for a year

will/won't + have been + -ing (future perfect continuous)

Positive: I'**ll have been** learn**ing** English for 3 years this time next month!
Negative: He **won't have been** liv**ing** there for long.
Question: How long **will** you **have been** do**ing** this job?

We use the future perfect continuous:
- to talk about how long an activity/situation will have been in progress by a specific time in the future. I'**ll have been** work**ing** here for 10 years next month.
- to focus on an activity in progress or a repeated action which leads up to a point in the future. When you arrive, I'll be very dirty because I'**ll have been** mend**ing** the car.
- to say what we believe is happening around now or was happening at a point in the past. He'**ll have been** watch**ing** the game last night, I'm sure.

ⓘ We do not usually use state verbs. NOT ~~I will have been knowing him~~

A Write the correct verb in the future perfect continuous.

come   cut   not/earn   get up   ~~work~~

1 At the end of next week we *'ll have been working* on this project for a year.

2 We _____ out here every day without fail.

3 We _____ at dawn for a very long time and we'll be tired of it by then.

4 Tomorrow night we'll be exhausted because we _____ wood all day.

5 I _____ money for over a year soon so I must get a job.

B Write the verbs in the future perfect or future perfect continuous.

1 At the end of this semester, Saskia *will have been studying* (study) at university for two years.

2 _____ (you/have) dinner before you get here or should I prepare something for you to eat?

3 Saturday week, I _____ (go out with) Cari for two years.

4 You _____ (drive) for over six hours soon. Why don't you stop for a rest?

5 I got home very late so my mother _____ (worry) about me all night.

6 Don't call me after six as I _____ (leave) by then.

7 I'll be exhausted by the time I cross the finish line as I _____ (run) for over four hours.

30 As far as I'm concerned

Attitude phrases

Finite clauses (which have a subject – *you*, *the fact* etc. – and a tense)	Non-finite clauses (including participle and *to*-infinitive phrases)
As far as I know, the shops are closed. Also: *as you know, as I said, I'm afraid, you know, the fact is that, believe it or not*	**To be honest,** I hated the film. Also: *all things considered, speaking from memory, to put it another way, strictly speaking*

Attitude phrases are used to:
- give your opinion/reaction. **Hopefully,** he'll win. Also: *worryingly, quite rightly, surprisingly, understandably, funnily enough*
- comment on the truth. **Actually,** that's not true. Also: *obviously, really, arguably*
- explain how you are speaking. **Frankly,** I think he's older than that. Also: *to my mind, in my opinion, seriously*
- generalise. **By and large,** the people are friendly. Also: *on the whole, as a rule*
- emphasise. **In fact,** I really enjoyed it. Also: *indeed, as a matter of fact*

A Complete these opinions with words from the box.

believe	~~fact~~	hopefully	know	mind	speaking
whole	worryingly				

1 'The ___*fact*___ is that there are too many cars on our streets.'
   '_____ it or not, more people are using public transport than ever before.'

2 'As you _____ , young people are making a nuisance of themselves late at nights.'
   'I don't agree. On the _____ , young people are very well behaved.'

3 'To my _____ , the number of homeless people is unacceptable.'
   '_____ , the situation will improve when the new houses are built.'

4 '_____ , the authorities spend too little money on our schools.'
   '_____ from memory, an extra million dollars was spent last year.'

B Underline the correct answer.

I'm writing to complain about the dirtiness of our city. (1) **As far as I know,/ Understandably,** none of the bins have been emptied for weeks and (2) **to put it another way,/not surprisingly,** the streets are filthy. Also, (3) **quite frankly,/all things considered,** when the collectors do come, they drop the contents of the bins everywhere and (4) **as I said,/as a rule,** don't even bother to pick the stuff up.

Also, tourists drop a lot of litter and, (5) **by and large,/strictly speaking,** it is left uncollected, giving an overall impression of dirtiness. (6) **Funnily enough,/In my opinion,** far more of our taxes should be spent on improving cleanliness and far less on councillors' salaries.

Test 3 (Units 21–30)

A Circle the correct answer.

1 I wish you **asked/had asked** me first! Why didn't you?

2 The car was bigger and **therefore/seeing that** it was more comfortable.

3 I'm capable **to look/of looking** after myself.

4 We'll **spend/be spending** the winter in Thailand. Come and visit us sometime.

5 Let's **come out/put on** the play in a London theatre.

6 He denied **him taking/having taken** my wallet.

7 Here are the keys. Can you **bring them back/bring back them** tomorrow?

8 By the end of the day I**'ve finished/'ll have finished** the report.

9 On July 1st we**'ll have been living/'ll be living** in this house for ten years.

10 There were some problems but **to put it another way/by and large** things went well.

[10]

B Write the verbs in the correct form.

1 If only I _____ (not/drink) so much coffee last night!

2 I wish you _____ (not/have) a meeting when I called. I wanted to talk to you.

3 There's no hope of ever _____ (get) this computer to work again.

4 This time tomorrow I _____ (sit) on the plane on my way to London.

5 _____ (you/see) Tom at work later? If so, can you give him this disk?

6 I persuaded her _____ (go) into hospital.

7 She apologised for _____ (be) late.

8 I _____ (already/finish) this job by tomorrow morning.

9 We _____ (work) here for 6 years next July.

10 By the time you see him, he _____ (hear) the news.

[10]

C Rewrite the words *in italics* using a phrasal verb. There is a clue in brackets.

1 He promised *to investigate the complaint.* (look) _____

2 His business has started *to become successful.* (off) _____

3 I'm sure they've *invented the whole story.* (up) _____

4 There's a lot of mess here. Can you *make it tidy?* (clear)

_____

5 Our house *is separate* from the town. (cut) _____

[5]

51

D Complete the sentences using the cues.

1 I was disappointed at (not/get/the job) ....
2 They denied (steal/the car) ....
3 I encouraged her (not/talk/to strangers) ....
4 Can you remind me (buy/some milk) .... ?
5 He insists on (play/music/late at night) ....

5

E Make one sentence using the expression in brackets.

1 I won't stay long. You're busy. (seeing as)

....

2 He can't vote. He's only seventeen. (and therefore)

....

3 The weather was awful. The concert was cancelled. (on account of)

....

4 We left a message. This is because there was no-one in. (so)

....

5 She played really well. It was her first game! (given that)

....

5

F Complete the sentences with one word.

1 As .... as I know, she's out today.
2 To .... honest, I don't like him very much.
3 On the ...., the conference went well.
4 All .... considered, she's quite a nice person.
5 Strictly ...., the book isn't a biography.

5

G Correct the mistakes.

1 If only I <u>studied</u> harder when I was younger. ....
2 We missed the last bus <u>therefore</u> we had to get a taxi. ....
3 He was annoyed <u>to be caught</u>. ....
4 Do you think you<u>'re still working</u> here in ten years' time? ....
5 I shall never forget the place where I <u>brought up</u>. ....
6 She suggested <u>to go</u> for a walk. ....
7 She was all alone. Nobody was <u>looking her after</u>. ....
8 I <u>have finished</u> this book by tomorrow. ....
9 He<u>'ll play</u> for United for ten years in July. ....
10 I thought we'd be late. <u>Hopefully</u>, we were early. ....

10

TOTAL

50

31 What's more, it's cheap

Linking ideas within a sentence	Linking ideas across sentences
• Addition: *as well as, in addition to, besides* • Time: *as, as soon as, at which point, until, while* • Contrast: *although, even though, whereas, while* • Reason and result: *as, since, so* • Purpose: *so that, (in order) to* **As well as** playing tennis, she goes swimming twice a week.	• Addition: *furthermore, moreover, what's more* • Time: *afterwards, beforehand, eventually, finally, meanwhile* • Contrast: *however, nevertheless, on the other hand* • Reason and result: *as a result, consequently, that's why, therefore* The house is in a perfect location. **What's more**, it's reasonably priced.

Linking back
To link back to something we said previously and to avoid repeating the same words we can use grammatical words such as pronouns (*she, it, them*), determiners (*that, these*), auxiliaries (*do*) and words like *so, such, there, then, not, one(s)* and *to*.   We could go but I'd prefer **not to**. (= not to go)

A Complete this theatre review with linking expressions from the box. Use each expression once.

> ~~although~~   as   as well as   however   in order to   moreover
> until   while

(1) *Although* now in its third year, this production of the musical *Chitty Chitty Bang Bang* is still attracting big crowds. As everyone knows, the story revolves around an inventor who buys an old magic racing car (2) .... please his children. (3) ...., the evil Baron Bomburst also wants the car and there are many attempts to capture it (4) .... eventually the Baron is defeated.

(5) .... many of the cast have changed in the last three years, what this production still has is the highly professional way in which it is directed, (6) ...., of course, the star of the show – the flying car! (7) ...., there are the same crazy machines and lots of energetic song and dance routines. This is delightful entertainment which pleases children and (8) .... pleases parents (9) .... they watch their young ones cry with laughter!

B Underline the most natural answer.

1 I go to musicals more often than Jan **goes/<u>does</u>**.

2 After Luke bought a ticket I **bought a ticket too/did too**.

3 Can we see *The Lion King*? **If we can't see *The Lion King*/If not**, can we see *Mamma Mia*?

4 Do you want to come? **If you want to come/If so**, give me a ring.

C Complete the gaps with one suitable word.

1 'We're meeting at 8.00.' 'OK, I'll see you _then_ .'

2 'Would you like to come round for dinner?' 'Yes, I'd love _____ .'

3 'I really enjoyed seeing Tokyo.' 'So _____ I.'

4 I also loved Osaka. Have you been _____ ?

5 Have you got a Japanese dictionary? If _____ , don't worry, I'll buy

_____ .

6 Claude finds learning Japanese as difficult as Serge _____ .

7 Felipe loves the Noh theatre and other _____ traditional Japanese arts.

D Rewrite these extracts from a letter, using the words in brackets. Use personal pronouns where appropriate.

1

> Probably the last thing you want to do in Tokyo is to spend time in the theatre. You really must go to see a Noh performance. A Noh performance combines dance, drama, music and poetry and is quite unique. You won't regret it. (*however, as, if*)

Probably the last thing you want to do in Tokyo is to spend time in the theatre. However, you really must go to see a Noh performance as it combines ...

2

> The performances are complex. The language used is hundreds of years old. The performers wear a mask. The performers' voices are rather difficult to hear. The audience often follow the performances with printed scripts. (*since, what's more, as a result*)

3

> I like the Noh play, *Kumasaka*. My favourite Noh play is *Sumidagawa*, in which a mother goes on a long journey to look for her lost son. The mother meets a ferryman at the Sumida River, who tells the mother that her son has been killed. By her son's graveside, a vision of her son appears and the mother tries to touch it. The vision vanishes. (*although, eventually, at which point*)

32 Everyone knows

Noun + singular verb

Everyone/Hardly anyone/(Almost) nobody knows the truth. (indefinite pronouns)
Each of the students/Every student has to be responsible.
One/More than one/Neither/None of these shops **sells** what I want.
Either of those ties **is** fine.
A hundred dollars/weeks/metres/kilos is not a lot. (quantities as a whole)
Tom, **as well as/together with/along with** his brother, **works** at the university.
The **news is** quite old. Also: *athletics, the United States* and usually *politics, economics*

ⓘ In spoken English, the plural verb is sometimes used after *neither/none of* and *either of*.

Noun + plural verb

Both Tom **and** Mary **work** at the university. (BUT Tom **but not** Mary **works** ...)
Clothes/Trousers/Scissors are cheap here. Also: *belongings, earnings, goods*
A number of things **are** not clear. Also: *a lot/couple/group of*
People say that food is expensive here. Also: *the police*

Noun + singular or plural verb

The government is divided over the issue. (a single body) **The government are** ... (as
individuals) Also: *family, committee, council, public, team, bank, class, club, crowd*

ⓘ **A lot of** the cars **are** sold in Italy. **A lot of** the film **is** very sad. **A lot of** coffee **is**
grown in Brazil. Also: *half/most/all (of), the rest of, the majority of*

A Underline the correct answer in these extracts from a political pamphlet.

1 Everyone **agree/<u>agrees</u>** that the current government
   has wasted our money.

2 Average earnings **is/<u>are</u>** going down again
   this year.

3 All of us **has/<u>have</u>** the right to live in a
   decent home.

4 Each of the government's promises about tax
   <u>was</u>/were broken last year.

5 People **is/<u>are</u>** fed up with hearing lies.

6 A number of things **needs/<u>need</u>** to be said about their policy on crime.

7 More than one of their ministers **<u>uses</u>/use** public money for private medical bills.

B Use a word from the box and *is/are/was/were* to complete the newspaper extracts.

| clothes   crowd   ~~police~~   team   the United States |

1 The _police are_ currently interviewing a new suspect in the murder case.
2 At the moment .... negotiating with Asia on trade policies.
3 He thought that this hockey .... the best one he had managed.
4 Last night the sell-out .... all there for one thing: to listen to the music.
5 Customers thought that the children's .... overpriced.

C Complete the news story with a suitable verb or auxiliary.

PASSENGERS WIN COMPENSATION FOR DELAYED FLIGHTS

No passenger (1) ....._is_..... happy when their plane is delayed, and yet most of us (2) .... spent many tiring hours at an airport waiting for a flight. Indeed, during the holiday season hardly any planes (3) .... on time and, to the extreme frustration of travellers, twelve hours (4) .... not an uncommon time to wait. One of the main reasons for the delays (5) .... that airlines allow a very short time for letting passengers off the plane and boarding new passengers. So today's news (6) .... good for travellers: from now on they will be able to claim up to 600 euros for a delayed flight. Both passengers and airlines (7) .... agreed for some time that something should be done and everyone except the airlines (8) .... said that compensation is a good idea. The Department of Transport (9) .... written to the airlines telling them they must comply with the ruling and the Traffic Users Council (10) .... expecting many cases to go to court.

D Write the verbs in the correct present form and use the cues to make sentences.

1 how much/those jeans/cost?
   How much do those jeans cost?

2 The majority/us/not/agree

3 Half/the workforce/be/women

4 Neither/them/know/what to do

5 None/the programmes on TV/be/worth watching

6 My brother/as well as my sister/live/in Scotland

33 It's time you left

It's (about/high) time (that)	+ past	
It's (about/high) time (that)	you **did** some work. (= it's urgent)	
It's time (for + object)	*to*-infinitive	
It's time (for him)	**to go** to bed.	

	suggest (+ *that*)	+ person	present/past/infinitive	
	suggest		**goes/doesn't go**	to the doctor. (informal)
I	**suggested** (that)	**he**	**went/didn't go/ should go**	
	suggest suggested		**(not) go/be sent**	to the Principal. (formal)

Also: *insist, ask, demand, recommend, it's important/essential/necessary/vital (that)*

A Write the verbs in the correct form.

1 I think it's about time he *settled down* (settle down) and *got* (get) married.

2 She insists that he .... (find) a good job first.

3 It's time they .... (start) saving some money.

4 It's essential that she .... (be) absolutely sure she could live with him.

5 I recommend he .... (buy) her an expensive engagement ring.

6 I told him it was vital that he .... (learn) to be more responsible.

7 I asked that her parents .... (not/be invited) to dinner just yet.

B Complete the sentences in an appropriate way.

1 You're so childish. It's high time you ....*grew up*........ .

2 It's very hot sitting here on the beach. I suggest we............................ .

3 The party's nearly over. It's time ....

4 The company owed me fifty dollars! I insisted that ....

5 There's a great job advertised in the newspaper. It's important you

....

6 He was lying. I demanded that I .... the truth.

7 He's been having driving lessons for ages. It's time ....

34 Being ill, he stayed in bed

Adverbial -ing clauses

Time

She stood outside **waiting for a bus**. (two things happened at the same time) **Having found/Finding a hotel** we looked for somewhere to eat. (one thing happened after the other) **On seeing her brother**, she screamed with delight. (= when she saw her brother)
Also: *after, before, since, while*

Cause, reason and result

Not feeling well, I decided to stay at home. (= I didn't feel well so ...)
By paying extra, she got seats in the front row.

Contrast

Despite meeting/having met her, I never got to know her well. Also: *in spite of, while*

ⓘNormally, the -*ing* clause must agree with the subject of the main clause. **Having no money, Tim couldn't lend me any.** (= Tim had no money) BUT **Tim having** no money, I paid for the meal. (different subjects)

ⓘ**Not feeling well**, it was best I went home. **There not being much time, we** rushed to the station.

A Look at the pictures and complete the sentences with an -*ing* clause.

1 He sat in the chair *reading a newspaper* .
2 Yesterday I cut myself _____ .
3 She hurt her arm _____ .
4 _____ , she went to bed.
5 _____ matches, I couldn't light a fire.

B Write the verbs in the correct form.

1 *Having copied* the letter, I gave it to the sales director. (copy)
2 They finished the job by _____ overtime. (work)
3 _____ to Malta, I knew what a beautiful country it is. (go)
4 Despite _____ her before, we got on very well. (not/meet)
5 On _____ the door, I realised I'd forgotten my briefcase. (reach)
6 While _____ through London, I got lost. (drive)
7 Ben _____ unemployed, his wife had to go out to work. (be)

C This story is about the detective Sherlock Holmes and his assistant, Dr Watson. Rewrite the sentences using an *-ing* clause.

1 Holmes predicted the arrival of a visitor and astonished Watson with his powers of observation.
   Predicting the arrival of a visitor, Holmes astonished Watson with his powers of observation.

2 The visitor introduced himself and asked them to investigate the death of his friend, Sir Charles Baskerville.
   After _____ them to investigate the death of his friend, Sir Charles Baskerville.

3 Sir Charles had seen a huge savage dog and died of shock.
   _____ of shock.

4 Holmes agreed to take the case and asked Watson to travel to Baskerville Hall.
   On _____ Baskerville Hall.

5 Watson wasn't a detective but when he arrived he started interviewing suspects.
   Despite _____ he started interviewing suspects.

6 Because he didn't know Holmes was also in the area he tried to solve the crime himself.
   Not _____ .

D Combine the sentences using a participle clause.

1 Sir Arthur Conan Doyle grew up in a cultured household. He loved to explore the world of books.
   Having grown up in a cultured household, Sir Arthur Conan Doyle loved to explore the world of books.

2 He had qualified as a doctor. However, in 1891 he became a full-time writer.
   In spite of _____ a full-time writer.

3 He was a scientist by training. However, he believed in fairies.
   Despite _____ .

4 He wrote several stories about Sherlock Holmes. Then in 1893 Conan Doyle decided to kill him off.
   After _____ to kill him off.

5 He returned to England from South Africa in 1902. He wrote *The Hound of the Baskervilles*.
   On _____ *The Hound of the Baskervilles*.

35 He talks as if he lived here

as if/though

	as if/though	+ clause/*-ing* clause/past participle/*to-* infinitive
She talks		**she knows/knew me**. (but she doesn't know me)
He looked at me		**he'd met me before**.
He smiled	**as if/though**	**enjoying himself**.
They collapsed		**exhausted**.
He phones daily		**to show** he cares. (perhaps he does)

ⓘ He **made as if to** leave. (= he seemed as if he was going to leave)

A Write the verbs in brackets in the correct form and add *as if* or *as though*.

1 Their General Manager acts just *as if he owned* (he/own) our company.

2 It seemed .... (we/lose) the contract.

3 Tim stood there .... (say) it wasn't his fault.

4 They talk to me almost .... (I/be) a junior employee, not the Chief Executive.

5 She started to shout .... (try) to frighten us into offering a better price.

6 In the break, they sounded .... (they/have) an argument.

7 He hesitated .... (confuse) about the details of the deal.

B Continue these sentences in an appropriate way.

1 They carried on talking as though *nothing had happened* .

2 The dog barked as if ....

3 What's the matter? You're looking at me as if ....

4 It's very quiet. It sounds as though ....

5 I don't feel very well. I feel as though ....

6 Why is he wearing those clothes? He's dressed as if ....

....

7 John stood up and made as if ....

8 She stared into the mirror as if ....

36 Built in 1400, it's now a museum

Passive past participle clauses

Time: **Once (When/Whenever) heard**, the tune is not forgotten. (= once it is heard)

Condition: **(If) Told** well, some jokes are very funny. (= if they are told well) **Unless kept** in the fridge, the fruit will go bad. (= unless it is kept)

Place: **Wherever played**, football is very popular. (= wherever it is played)

Cause, reason, result: I applied for the job, **convinced** that I could do it. (= because I was convinced) **The job finished, they** went for lunch. (two subjects: **The job** was finished so **they** …)

Contrast: **Although attacked** by the media, he refused to resign. (= although he was attacked)

ⓘ Past participle clauses can also be used as adjectives. Every night he comes home **exhausted** after a day's work. (= and he is exhausted)

A Join the sentences.

1 Tate Modern is a huge gallery of modern art. It was opened in 2000.
   Opened in 2000, Tate Modern is a huge gallery of modern art.

2 The London Eye dominates the skyline. It is located by the River Thames.
   _____ dominates the skyline.

3 The *Cutty Sark* is now dry-docked in Greenwich. It was first launched in 1869.
   _____ dry-docked in Greenwich.

4 The London Dungeon is now a top attraction. It was originally built as a prison.
   _____ a top attraction.

5 The Crown Jewels are on display in the Tower of London. They are used for important state occasions.
   _____ in the Tower of London.

B Rewrite the sentences using a past participle clause.

1 Hamleys Toy Shop is intended for children but it delights many adults.
   Although _intended for adults, Hamleys Toy Shop_ delights many adults.

2 If you don't pay for tickets for West End shows in advance, they can be very expensive.
   Unless _____ very expensive.

3 Tourists should try to find a policeman any time they're lost.
   Whenever _____ a policeman.

4 People never forget the view from Waterloo Bridge from the moment they see it.
   Once _____ is never forgotten.

37 If I was him, I'd have left

Mixed conditionals

Mixed conditionals combine the verb forms from two different conditional patterns.
For unreal past situations with an imaginary result in the present:

past perfect simple/continuous	+ *would/could/might* + verb
If you **hadn't made** a mess (but you did)	this place **would look** a lot tidier now.

For unreal present situations with an imaginary result in the past:

past simple/continuous	+ *would/could/might have* + verb
If I **were** a nicer person (but I'm not),	**I'd have lent** her some money. (in the past)

A Write the verbs in the correct form.

1 If they _hadn't built up_ (not/build up) so many debts, their financial position
would be (be) a lot healthier now.

2 Their costs .... (be) a lot lower now if they
.... (restructure) the company last year.

3 If I .... (be) one of their current investors, I
.... (go) to that shareholders' meeting last night.

4 If they .... (invest) more when they started they
.... (make) a profit now.

5 The Chief Executive .... (still/work) here now if he
.... (not/make) so many silly mistakes.

6 If they .... (not/lose) some of their best developers, they
.... (still/be) a very successful company.

B Write mixed conditional sentences using the information given.

1 I always work very hard. I was able to run the company by myself.
If _I didn't always work very hard, I wouldn't have been able to_ run the
company by myself.

2 I didn't trust him. We are not working together now.
If .... together now.

3 I went into business when I was very young. I am rich and successful today.
If .... rich and successful today.

4 I'm well-off. I was able to buy a large house in the Bahamas.
If .... a large
house in the Bahamas.

5 I understand how business works. I was brought up in a business environment.
If .... how business works.

38 Little does he know

Inversion after negative introductory expressions

negative expression	+ auxiliary	+ subject	
Never	have	I	seen such a mess.
No sooner/hardly/Barely	had	we	arrived **than** it started to rain.

Never again will we trust them.
Under no circumstances/On no account should you go out alone.
At no time/Not once/On one occasion did he apologise.
Little does he realise how serious the situation is.
Only now does he appreciate what I said. **Only when** it got dark did I feel frightened.
Also: *Only later, Only then, Only after that, Only once*
Not until I left did I realise my mistake. Also: *Not only … but (also), Not for one minute, Not since*

A Write the verbs in the correct form.

1 Little *did I realise* _____ (I/realise) how unsafe the place was.

2 No sooner _____ (I/climb inside) than I heard a strange sound.

3 Not for one minute _____ (I/expect) the wall to collapse.

4 Never _____ (I/be) in such a dangerous situation.

5 Luckily, at no time _____ (the cave/get) completely flooded.

6 Only when the rescuers arrived _____ (I/feel) safe.

7 Only now _____ (I/realise) how lucky I was.

B Rewrite the sentences from an interview starting with the underlined word.

1 I did <u>not</u> get a chance to rest until I got home.
 Not until I got home did I get a chance to rest.

2 I have <u>never</u> in my life been so scared.

_____

3 I shouldn't have gone in there <u>under</u> any circumstances.

_____

4 I will <u>not</u> only go with another person in future, but I will also make sure the cave is safe first.

_____

5 I will <u>never</u> be so silly again!

_____

39 What he did was ...

Emphasising important information

what clause	+ *be*
What surprises me	**is** his age. (focus on the subject: **his age**)
What I needed	**was** a holiday. (focus on the object: **a holiday**)
What I did	**was** (to) leave the company. (focus on the verb: **leave**)
What happened	**was** (that) the car broke down. (focus on the sentence)

ⓘ Also: **All/The (one) thing** I know/need/want is ... **All that happened was** (that) ...

ⓘ Instead of putting other *wh-* clauses at the beginning we prefer:
The place where we lived has been pulled down. Also: **The person/people who** ...
The reason why/that ...

It + be + wh-/that

It was Tom/him (*he* – formal) **who** wrote the awful letter. (focus on the subject)
It was an awful letter **that** Tom/he wrote. (focus on the object)
It was while Tom was away **that** he wrote that letter. (focus on the adverbial clause)

A Complete the sentences.

1 Franklin was a successful printer but science interested him more.
Franklin was a successful printer but what *interested him more was* science.

2 He wanted to discover the nature of electricity.
What he _____ the nature of electricity.

3 He flew a kite with a wire and key attached during a thunderstorm.
What he _____ during a thunderstorm.

4 At first, bits of string on the kite stood up stiffly. Nothing else happened.
At first, all _____ on the kite stood up stiffly.

5 A spark flew between the key and his hand. This happened next.
Then what _____ between the key and the hand.

6 He had proved that lightning and electricity are the same force.
What he _____ are the same force.

B Join the two halves of these sentences about explorers.

1 The people who   a reached the South Pole first was Roald Amundsen.

2 The place where   b first discovered Hawaii were the Polynesians.

3 The person who   c David Livingstone is famous for is his exploration of Africa.

4 The reason why   d Alfred Gibson died is now called the Gibson Desert.

5 The thing that   e Erik Thorvaldsson was called Erik the Red was because he had red hair.

C Read this encyclopaedia extract and correct the sentences.

GREEK HISTORIANS

The world's first historian was Herodotus (c.485–c.429BC), who, having travelled widely throughout Asia Minor, wrote about the wars between the Greeks and Persians. Called the 'father of history' by the Roman statesman Cicero, his *Histories* are still widely read today. Another Greek historian was Thucydides (c.460–c.395BC), whose story of the war fought between Athens and Sparta up to c.404 is less romantic and less well-known today. The story of that war was continued by Xenephon (c.430–c.354BC), a student of the philosopher Socrates, in his book *Hellenica*.

1 Herodotus wrote about the wars between the Greeks and Trojans.

No, it was *the wars between the Greeks and Persians that he wrote about* .

2 He travelled widely throughout the Far East.

No, it was _____ .

3 Socrates called him the 'father of history'.

No, it was _____ .

4 Thucydides was born in c.560.

No, it was _____ .

5 Thucydides is still widely read today.

No, it is _____ .

6 Xenephon wrote about the Athens–Sparta war in his book *Histories*.

No, it was _____ .

D Complete these sentences for you.

1 What I'd like to do when I get older is _____ *write a novel* _____ .

2 The thing I'd most like to do in the next year is _____ .

3 The reason why I'd like to _____ is _____ .

4 The place where I like to _____ is _____ .

5 What I do when I'm bored is _____ .

6 It's _____ that I dislike most about modern life.

7 The person who _____ me the most is _____ .

40 There goes John

A Complete the sentences.

Danger In The Tropics

1 The heat was so intense that it was hard to sleep.
   So _intense was the heat_ that it was hard to sleep.

2 Her anxiety was such that she didn't sleep for long.
   Such .... that she didn't sleep for long.

3 The storm was so terrible that it felt like the end of he world.
   So .... that it felt like the end of the world.

4 There was such chaos on the streets that she was afraid to go out.
   Such .... that she was afraid to go out.

5 She was so unsure of her safety that she tried to phone the Embassy.
   So .... that she tried to phone the Embassy.

B Rewrite these sentences to make them more dramatic. Move the underlined words in front of the subject and make any other necessary changes.

1 A note from his wife was <u>attached to the key</u>.
   Attached to the key was a note from his wife.

2 The door suddenly opened and a crazy dog rushed <u>out</u>.

   ....

3 Someone I recognised was <u>waiting for me in the cafe</u>.

   ....

4 Knowing that he used to be my best friend was <u>the worst thing of all</u>.

   ....

Test 4 (Units 31–40)

A Circle the correct answer.

1 **Moreover,/In addition to** her jewellery, some of her money was missing.
2 Athletics **isn't/aren't** my favourite sport.
3 We recommend he **wasn't giving/not be given** the prize.
4 Despite **I felt/feeling** tired, I still stayed up till midnight.
5 He talks all the time as if **to show/he shows** he's not nervous.
6 Unless **swallowing/swallowed** with a lot of water, the pills taste awful.
7 If the train **weren't/hadn't been** delayed, we'd be there by now.
8 Never **have I seen/I have seen** anything so beautiful.
9 What **was happened next/happened next was** that the police arrived.
10 So **hot was it/it was hot** that I could hardly breathe.

10

B Write the verbs in the correct form.

1 Every one of them _____ (be) here before.
2 Look! A number of people _____ (climb) up the tower.
3 It's about time you _____ (change) your diet.
4 _____ (take off) his shoes, he went upstairs.
5 Although _____ (feel) rather silly, she refused to say sorry.
6 He behaved as though nothing _____ (happen).
7 She narrowed her eyes as if _____ (try) to see something in the distance.
8 _____ (lose) for many years, the letters suddenly turned up.
9 If they _____ (not/live) so far away now you could have gone round to see them.
10 At no time _____ (he/ever/thank) me for what I did for him.

10

C Complete the gaps with one word.

1 Would you like a cup of tea? If _____, I'll get you _____ .
2 _____ me, the only other people there were Tom and Fiona.
3 _____ was extraordinary was that he was only eighteen years old!
4 _____ was on Saturday that we went to London, not Friday.
5 The _____ I like most in the evenings is a hot bath.

5

D Make one sentence using the correct expression in brackets.

1 Some people look forward to retirement. Others can't bear the idea.
(nevertheless/while)

....

2 They help people in need. They also raise money for charity. (as well as/as well)

....

3 I didn't have a ticket. I couldn't get into the concert. (not/although)

....

4 I've lived in London. Cambridge seems very quiet to me. (on/after)

....

5 He doesn't do a very good job. He is paid a lot of money. (unless/despite)

....

5

E Rewrite the sentences starting with the word given.

1 People like that should be put in prison. Such ....

2 When they met, the two men shook hands. On ....

3 I'm feeling ill because I ate too much. If ....

4 I'm good at my job so I got promoted. If ....

5 The trouble started not long after we arrived. Hardly ....

6 He's always late and he's very lazy. Not only ....

7 He took a lot more exercise. What ....

8 They met when he was on holiday. It ....

9 The last question was much more difficult. Much ....

10 He was so strong he could pull a bus. Such ....

10

F Correct the mistakes.

1 He likes cars more than I <u>do like cars</u>. ....

2 Five euros <u>aren't</u> very much. ....

3 It's time for him <u>that he went</u> to bed. ....

4 While drinking a cup of coffee, <u>my dog sat with me</u> by the fire. ....

5 He smiled as if <u>to know</u> me. ....

6 Once <u>opening</u>, keep the medicine in the fridge. ....

7 We wouldn't be friends again if he <u>didn't say</u> sorry. ....

8 Not until much later <u>I found out</u> the truth. ....

9 <u>Who</u> discovered penicillin is Alexander Fleming. ....

10 Inside the letter <u>a cheque was</u>. ....

10

TOTAL

50

68

Time and tense

Present time

Present simple	• things that are always true • things we see as permanent • things that happen regularly • state verbs (*feel, think*)	I **come** from Canada. She **lives** in France. He **always sleeps** late. I **like** coffee.
Present continuous	• things happening now • temporary situations • changing situations • to emphasise how often	Look! It**'s raining**. He**'s studying** science. It**'s getting** dark. He**'s always** smiling.
Past simple/continuous	• unreal situations	If I **were** you ... I wish I **had** a sister. It's time we **were going**.
Future continuous	• predictions about something happening now	Don't go in! He**'ll be having** lunch.

Future time

will	• predictions when we are certain • spontaneous decisions (offers, promises, requests)	I'm sure they**'ll be** late. OK. I**'ll carry** that bag for you.
be going to	• predictions based on what we can see now • decisions that we have already made (plans/intentions)	It's cloudy. It**'s going to rain**. I**'m going to buy** a new car.
Present continuous	• arrangements	I**'m taking** my driving test tomorrow.
Present simple	• public timetables/programmes • after time expressions	The bus **leaves** in half an hour. I'll see you **when you get back**.
Future continuous	• temporary activity going on at a certain time • part of a schedule of arrangements • part of a routine • to ask about intentions	This time tomorrow I**'ll be sleeping**. We**'ll be moving** to Germany in July. I**'ll be seeing** her on Friday as usual. **Will you be using** your car later?
Future perfect	• predictions about future completed actions	He**'ll have gone** before you get back.
be to	• formal official arrangements	The Queen **is to visit** Canada later.

Past time as seen from the present

Present perfect simple	• recent past action that affects the present	Oh, no! I've left the tickets at home.
	• general experiences	She's travelled all over the world.
	• unfinished time period	I've been abroad twice this year.
Present perfect continuous	• continuing/recently finished temporary actions started in the past	I'm tired. I've been playing tennis.
	• to emphasise how long	He's been waiting for ages.
Future perfect	• to say what we believe has happened before now	He'll have left by now.

Past time

Past simple	• completed actions/states at a specific time in the past	I went to Madrid last Thursday.
	• details of news events	He's arrived. his plane landed at 6.00.
Past continuous	• unfinished temporary actions	At 8.30, we were walking home.
	• general description	The sun was shining.
	• a long action interrupted by a shorter action	We were having lunch when the telephone rang.
Past perfect	• events/actions before a past time	By the time we got there the plane had left.
	• unreal situations	If I'd seen him, I'd have told him.
Past perfect continuous	• temporary activity in progress up to a specific time in the past	Before I went to Rome, I'd been living in Moscow for 3 years.
used to	• past habits/states	She used to live in Athens.
would	• past habits	He would always stay home on Fridays.
was going to	• unfulfilled plans/intentions	I was going to email her but I forgot.
	• past predictions	I thought it was going to be really cold.

Punctuation

Punctuation mark	Use	Example
Apostrophe '	• to show possession	Tom's jo... a boys' s... the men's... plural)
	• for contractions	It's late.
Capital letter **G**	• to begin a sentence	**H**e wrote to me.
	• names, pronoun *I*, countries, nationalities, cities, days of the week, months, titles	**B**ob and **I**, **B**razil/**B**razilian, **L**ondon, **F**riday, **M**ay, **T**he **T**imes
Colon :	• to introduce a list	There are three reasons: first, ...
	• before an explanation/extra information/example/quotation	She was worried: it was getting dark.
Comma ,	• for items in a list	I bought apples, pears(,) and bananas.
	• to divide groups of words	He got up, had a shower(,) and left.
	• around non-defining relative clauses and other inserted phrases	My father, who lives in Wales, is 83. She is, however, very intelligent.
	• before question tags	It's late, isn't it?
	• after *if*/time clauses and other introductory phrases	If I were you, I'd resign. When it rains, I take an umbrella. Besides, he's not a very nice person. Feeling tired, he went to bed.
	• in direct speech	'It's late,' he said. He said, 'It's late.'
Dash –	• to separate extra information (informal)	The second man – Tom – was also late.
Exclamation mark !	• for emotional emphasis	What a lovely day!
Full stop .	• to show the end of a sentence	I'm very tired.
	• abbreviations, decimals, prices, time	e.g. 3.50% £2.99 4.30 am
Question mark ?	• after a direct question	Are you happy?
Semi-colon ;	• to separate two main clauses with a link in meaning	It was dark; it was getting late.
Speech marks " " ' '	• to show exact words	"I'll help you," he said. 'I'll help you,' he said.

...have 3 are getting 4 hadn't seen
5 've been working 6 'm trying
7 Do you know 8 's having

B 1 haven't met 2 've been 3 had left
4 've just found 5 have you known; 've
been 6 hadn't spoken

C 2 'd grown 3 was studying 4 'd never
thought 5 'd had to 6 had been work-
ing/was working 7 've been working
8 've travelled 9 've had 10 've been
reading/read 11 'm getting 12 've always
liked 13 'm thinking 14 've never
taken/never took

Unit 2

A 2 needs painting/to be painted
3 have/get it cleaned 4 needs tidying/to
be tidied 5 get/have them fitted 6 need
decorating/to be decorated

B Answers will vary.

Unit 3

A 2 can 3 must 4 shouldn't 5 could
6 couldn't 7 should 8 can

B 2 should/ought to 3 mustn't 4 must
5 May/Could/Can; can't 6 could/can

C 2 might not be 3 will cure 4 will
continue 5 can get 6 may/might agree
7 can/could use 8 will give

D 2 I may/might go out later. 3 My friends
must (will) be wondering 4 This can't be
the right road.

Unit 4

A 2 got; 'd been travelling 3 reached;
looked; realised 4 was getting; 'd been
planning; went (had gone); started ('d
started) 5 was walking; went; shouted;
was; 'd broken

B 2 didn't see/wouldn't see/didn't use to
see 3 used to live; had 4 spent/would
spend 5 used to go/went/would go

C 2 was feeling (felt/'d been feeling) 3 got
on 4 'd been waiting ('d waited) 5 was
finally leaving 6 used to fly (flew/'d
flown/would fly) 7 was (used to be/had
been) 8 would have to (had to/had had
to/used to have to) 9 had taken off (took
off) 10 told 11 had 12 started 13 saw
14 wondered 15 were standing by
16 didn't know 17 had fallen off 18 felt
19 came 20 were crying 21 had made
22 was injured (had been injured)
23 caught

D Answers will vary.

Unit 5

A 2 who used 3 which 4 albatross, which
is 5 world where 6 whom

B 2 whose 3 whom 4 which 5 who

C 2 from a second-hand bookshop, some of
whose books 3 (Superstitions), many of
which are based on old ideas about
magic, are beliefs about 4 (Superstitions),
about which many books have been
written, are 5 (Actors and sailors), whose
occupations are very insecure, have
6 a Japanese girl who believes that it is
bad luck to sleep 7 (Brazilians), who have
many ancient superstitions, believe

D 2 that man Maria's talking to 3 on which
the film is based (which the film is based
on), Che Guevara describes his journey to
Peru on a motorbike
4 two good friends, both of whom I see
regularly 5 many trips to Brazil, the most
recent of which was in July

Unit 6

A 2 might have been 3 can't have moved
4 could they have made; must have used
5 Could the Romans have built; couldn't
have (done)

B 2 might have 3 must have 4 must have
been 5 can't have slept

C 2 couldn't have killed 3 must have
panicked 4 might have had 5 may have
felt 6 Could they have been

D 2 The bodies may/might not have been
3 There can't have been a seaquake
4 Could there have been 5 Everyone must
have been feeling 6 Could it have been
raining 7 No, it couldn't (can't) have been

Unit 7

A 2 grew 3 go 4 end up 5 become 6 get

B 2 come 3 become 4 go 5 fall 6 get

C Answers will vary. 2 … get dressed at
… 3 … like to become famous. 4 … go
crazy (if) I had to … 5 (and) it proved to
be very useful.

Unit 8

A 2 shouldn't have bought 3 ought to have
called 4 might have told 5 Shouldn't the
assistant have given; should have (done)
6 could have got

B 2 should have booked 3 should have
gone 4 shouldn't have bought
5 shouldn't have been listening (shouldn't
have listened) 6 should have put
7 should have come

Unit 9

A 2 starring 3 called 4 costing 5 sitting
6 being considered 7 described

B 2 given to her by her father, are now
worth a lot of money 3 made by Caruso,
was my mother's favourite 4 born in
Naples in 1873, was the eighteenth of
twenty-one children/the eighteenth of
twenty-one children, was born …
5 interested in Caruso's life, visited his
home in Italy

Unit 10

A 2 Apart from 3 Besides 4 Apart from
5 except for 6 apart from; her 7 book

B 2 Apart from/Except for a few volunteers
3 apart from/except for the main speaker
4 except for/apart from when the coffee
runs out 5 Besides/Apart from the
lectures

Test 1 (Units 1–10)

A 1 had already started 2 get our photo
taken 3 must 4 used to 5 whom
6 couldn't have 7 get 8 should 9 hurt
10 except for

B 1 can't have been 2 must be 3 shouldn't
have spoken 4 must have taken 5 might
be/may be/could be 6 should be
7 might/may not have 8 shouldn't have
been talking 9 could sing 10 mustn't tell

C 1 whose 2 which 3 whom 4 which
5 who

D 1 was having 2 've been 3 'd been
making 4 did you first arrive
5 checking/to be checked 6 'm thinking
(was thinking) 7 hadn't met 8 fitted
9 seems 10 've been trying

E 1 He took no notice of the telephone
ringing on his desk. 2 The subject being
discussed at the meeting is climate change.
3 A lot of people invited to the party
arrived late. 4 The students sitting at the
back couldn't see a thing. 5 The man
given an award for bravery died last night.

F 1 moved 2 get my laptop repaired 3 can't
4 'd been travelling 5 which 6 Could
7 came 8 oughtn't to have driven
9 suggested/which were suggested
10 Besides/Apart from

Unit 11

A 2 had defeated; mightn't have conquered
3 would have happened; had thought
4 hadn't shot; mightn't have been
5 mightn't have been assassinated; hadn't
been travelling

B 2 'd (could/might) have passed
3 would you have studied; might (could)
have studied 4 'd known 5 hadn't
recommended; might (would/could)
have tried 6 'd gone; wouldn't (mightn't)
have met

C 2 If she hadn't saved up her school dinner
money, she wouldn't (mightn't) have been
able to buy a boat. 3 She wouldn't have
become a sailor if she'd decided to study to
be a vet. 4 She wouldn't have won the
Young Sailor of the Year Award if she hadn't
sailed around Britain single-handed. 5 If
she hadn't had a good boat, she wouldn't
have broken the round-the-world record by
31 hours. 6 If the boat's generator had
failed, the navigational equipment wouldn't
have worked.

D 2 If my alarm hadn't rung this morning, I'd have been late for work. 3 If you'd asked politely, I'd have lent you my car. 4 If we'd saved more money, we might have been able to afford a holiday abroad. 5 If you'd read the instructions, you wouldn't have broken the washing machine. 6 If you hadn't reminded me, I'd have forgotten to pay my tax bill.

Unit 12

A 2 on getting 3 for wanting 4 for suspecting 5 of posting 6 of taking 7 for making 8 for keeping

B 2 (about) the staff against coming in late in the mornings 3 to the manager about being overworked 4 you from leaving 5 you against asking your boss for a reference (you not to ask)

Unit 13

A 2 The richer; the fewer 3 the better 4 not so much 5 than 6 more confused

B 2 she looks younger 3 she gets, the more attractive she gets 4 than successful at work 5 he works, the less he wants to work.

Unit 14

A 2 should be stored 3 must be switched off 4 can be filled in

B 2 get lost 3 get hurt 4 got stuck 5 got taken away; (got) examined

C 2 could have been created (a) 3 can't have been carried out (d) 4 might have been broken off (b) 5 could have been worn away (c)

D 2 to be met 3 getting lost 4 to be taken 5 to be shown 6 being looked after

E 2 must have been transferred 3 being offered 4 might be given 5 shouldn't be forgotten 6 got elected 7 to be (being) undervalued 8 to get overlooked 9 being asked 10 got selected 11 to be given 12 should be told 13 should have been told

Unit 15

A 2 to hear; moving 3 having; not to have 4 to get 5 finding 6 to go

B 2 have any difficulty (in) finding 3 wrong of Tania to refuse 4 busy writing 5 no good at making

Unit 16

A 2 it was assumed 3 there were thought to be 4 Our leading charities are said to be 5 is believed to have welcomed 6 the public were asked to give 7 it has been shown 8 this is not expected to happen

B 2 is feared that 3 has been suggested that 4 is expected that

C 2 are thought to have been 3 was rumoured to have failed 4 is believed to have been 5 is reported to haunt 6 is considered to be/to have been

D 2 (There) are estimated to be 20,000 refugees; (It) is estimated that there are 20,000 refugees 3 (It) is reported that the software company is making …; (The software company) is reported to be making 4 (The killer) is known to have committed …; (It) is known that that the killer has committed 5 (There) is believed to have been a big earthquake; (It) is believed that there has been a big earthquake

Unit 17

A 2 would have won; hadn't been 3 wins; 'll 4 are; will 5 'd; had

B 2 Should 3 Had 4 Were 5 Should

C 2 he hadn't begun; he wouldn't have become 3 He'd have got; he hadn't been 4 there's; people still say 5 He wouldn't have been; hadn't refused

D 2 But for her dedication, Kelly Holmes wouldn't have won 3 What if I went in for the marathon 4 Suppose Cathy Freeman were still running today. Would she … 5 'll do well provided that you love 6 … felt unwell. Otherwise she'd have finished

E 2 'd had 3 's 4 find 5 kept 6 'd be
7 'd practised 8 'd have won

Unit 18

A 2 while 3 However 4 in spite of 5 Even
so

B 2 Although his guardian wanted him to
follow a different career 3 In spite of
being only (In spite of the fact that he
was only) 17, he joined 4 wrote about
domestic dramas, whereas Conrad wrote
about
5 Famous writers praised his novels.
Nevertheless, at first they weren't …

Unit 19

A 2 particularly 3 even 4 just 5 simply
6 Just

B 2 He couldn't even take the time to
phone me 3 I only eat toast for breakfast
4 We don't go out very often, mainly
because we haven't got …

Unit 20

A 2 Starting 3 That you survived 4 How
much more we should spend
5 Borrowing money 6 Not to have
expanded

B 2 Comparing what we do … is wrong.
3 Finding the right staff takes 4 To
expand (Expanding) overseas is 5 That
we might fail is always 6 What our next
product is going to be is a

Test 2 (Units 11–20)

A 1 had set 2 for being 3 older; happier
4 be banned 5 to leave 6 to be 7 Should
8 whereas 9 mostly 10 What

B 1 'd gone; 'd have enjoyed 2 might have
been cured; had been called 3 applying
4 arrested 5 being told 6 to see 7 was
announced 8 Had I known 9 is delayed
10 Learning

C 1 Forgive me for asking 2 There's more
than enough food 3 There's no need for
you to worry. 4 She's a particularly clever
student. 5 Just help yourself.

D 1 for 2 on 3 so; as 4 and 5 been 6 of
7 Were 8 Although 9 even 10 Only

E 1 If we'd caught the train, we wouldn't
have been looking for a taxi half the
night./We wouldn't have been looking
for a taxi half the night if we … 2 I still
enjoyed myself, despite the bad weather
(despite the weather being bad/despite
the fact that the weather was bad)/
Despite the … 3 Even though he's got a
good job, he still complains./He still
complains even though … 4 But for his
rudeness (But for him being rude) I
would have enjoyed the evening./I would
have enjoyed the evening but for …
5 That people learn in different ways is
not a new idea. It's not a new idea that …

F 1 'd taken 2 (from) crying 3 expensive it
is 4 to be put 5 to hear 6 is hoped
7 get 8 working/having worked 9 I'm
not especially keen 10 I spoke to

Unit 21

A 2 'd played 3 'd passed 4 hadn't been
lying 5 'd had 6 hadn't stopped

B 2 'd brought 3 had 4 hadn't 5 hadn't
been driving 6 would read

C Answers will vary.

Unit 22

A 2 That's why 3 because of 4 therefore
5 Due to 6 In view of 7 Seeing as

B 2 d 3 e 4 b 5 a

C 2 You should get plenty of sleep since it's
3 You shouldn't eat too much junk food
seeing as/that it's full 4 The doctor told
Susie to take regular exercise on account
of 5 Tom's health improved because there
was more fruit 6 My mother wanted to
keep her brain active and therefore she/
… active. Therefore, she

D Answers will vary. 2 I didn't have much
money. Therefore, I had to stay in a cheap
hotel. 3 I couldn't go for long walks as it
was raining. 4 I was bored. That's why I
decided to get a taxi and go window
shopping. 5 The town was very lively
due to the fact that there was a street
festival going on. 6 Everyone was very
friendly. Consequently, I made lots of
friends.

Unit 23

A 2 about (us) losing 3 of him closing 4 on journalists working 5 of things getting

B 2 at hearing 3 for making sure 4 of increasing 5 at/about having to 6 of writing 7 of not doing 8 for making

Unit 24

A 2 'll be going 3 Will you be needing 4 'll be working 5 'll be seeing 6 'll be thinking

B 2 'll send 3 'll be having 4 're going to be coming 5 should be waiting 6 Will you be going

C 1 'll be 2 Will you email; Will you be working; 'll send 3 will you be doing; 'll probably be getting 4 will be taking off; 'll put 5 won't be staying; 'll come 6 Will you be using; 'll have to

D 2 'll be; 'll be earning 3 'll be living; 'll have 4 'll be taking; 'll still be living 5 'll be; 'll be spending

E Answers will vary.

Unit 25

A 2 passed away 3 was brought up 4 came out 5 set up 6 put on 7 take off 8 is thought of 9 look up to 10 is cut off 11 looks into

B 2 have been put on 3 will be set up 4 were cut off 5 'm thought of

Unit 26

A 2 convinced 3 mention 4 persuaded 5 refused 6 regretted 7 apologised

B 2 suggested taking/suggested that we took 3 advised us to forget/advised us that we should forget 4 reminded Tania not to forget/reminded Tania that she shouldn't forget 5 admitted being/admitted that he was 6 insisted on us negotiating/insisted that we negotiate

C 2 He admitted damaging/that he had damaged the hard disk. 3 He explained to me that he didn't really understand the problem. 4 He apologised to me for ruining the machine. 5 He offered to lend me his laptop. 6 I suggested that he bought me a new one. 7 I reminded him that I had lost a lot of data. 8 I didn't/won't invite him to stay with me again!

D 2 He complained that I was always playing my music too loudly. 3 She insisted on paying./She insisted that she paid. 4 She encouraged me to try for a place at university. 5 We agreed not to talk about it again./He agreed with me that we shouldn't talk about it again.

Unit 27

A 2 Add in the chopped celery, red pepper, onion and carrot. 3 fill it up 4 Stir in the cumin seeds. 5 Heat up the stove./Heat the stove up. 6 boil over 7 cut down on calories

B 2 has gone off 3 've run out of red caviar 4 take the skins off 5 throw them away 6 Clear the kitchen up

Unit 28

A 2 will have sold 3 will have cost 4 will have created 5 will not have had 6 will have changed

B Answers will vary. 2 … we will have built 30 new schools. 3 … we will have reduced street crime. 4 … we will have increased the minimum wage. 5 … we will have cut the price of train fares.

C 2 'll have met 3 'll see; 'll be talking 4 will have finished 5 'll already have had; won't be 6 'll be driving 7 'll already have left

D Answers will vary. 2 might have run out 3 won't have been eradicated 4 will have ruined 5 should have been found 6 will have landed

Unit 29

A 2 'll have been coming 3 'll have been getting up 4 'll have been cutting 5 won't have been earning

B 2 Will you have had 3 'll have been going out with 4 'll have been driving 5 will have been worrying 6 'll have left 7 'll have been running

Unit 30

A 1 Believe 2 know; whole 3 mind; Hopefully 4 Worryingly; Speaking

B 2 not surprisingly 3 quite frankly 4 as a rule 5 by and large 6 In my opinion

Test 3 (Units 21–30)

A 1 had asked 2 therefore 3 of looking 4 be spending 5 put on 6 having taken 7 bring them back 8 'll have finished 9 'll have been living 10 by and large

B 1 hadn't drunk 2 hadn't been having 3 getting 4 'll be sitting 5 Will you be seeing (Are you seeing) 6 to go 7 being 8 'll have already finished 9 'll have been working ('ll have worked) 10 'll have heard

C 1 to look into the complaint 2 to take off 3 made up the whole story/made the whole story up 4 clear it up 5 is cut off

D 1 not getting the job 2 stealing the car/ that they had stolen the car 3 not to talk to strangers 4 to buy some milk 5 playing music late at night

E 1 Seeing as you're busy I won't stay long./I won't stay long seeing as … 2 He's only seventeen and therefore (he) can't vote. 3 The concert was cancelled on account of the awful weather/the weather being awful./On account of the awful weather, the … 4 There was no-one in so we left a message. 5 Given that it was her first game, she played really well./She played really well given that …

F 1 far 2 be 3 whole 4 things 5 speaking

G 1 'd studied 2 bus and therefore we/ bus. Therefore, we 3 at being caught 4 'll still be working 5 was brought up 6 going 7 looking after her 8 'll have finished 9 'll have been playing 10 actually

Unit 31

A 2 in order to 3 However 4 until 5 While 6 as well as 7 Moreover 8 therefore 9 as

B 2 did too 3 If not 4 If so

C 2 to 3 did 4 there 5 not; one 6 does 7 such

D Answers will vary. 1 … dance, drama and music and is quite unique. If you do, you won't regret it. 2 The performances are complex since the language used is hundreds of years old. What's more, the performers wear a mask and their voices are rather difficult to hear. As a result, the audience often follow the performances with printed scripts. 3 Although I like the Noh play *Kumasaka*, my favourite (one) is *Sumidagawa*, in which a mother goes on a journey to look for her lost son. Eventually, she meets a ferryman at the Sumida River, who tells her that her son has been killed. By his graveside, a vision of her son appears and she tries to touch it, at which point it vanishes.

Unit 32

A 2 are 3 have 4 was 5 are 6 need 7 uses

B 2 the United States is 3 team was (were) 4 crowd were (was) 5 clothes were

C 2 have 3 leave 4 is 5 is 6 is 7 have 8 has 9 has 10 is (are)

D 2 The majority of us don't agree. 3 Half the workforce are women. 4 Neither of them knows (know) what to do. 5 None of the programmes on TV is (are) worth watching. 6 My brother, as well as my sister, lives in Scotland.

Unit 33

A 2 finds (must find) 3 started 4 is/be
5 buys/buy 6 learnt/learn 7 isn't
invited/not be invited

B Answers will vary. 2 go/should go 3 we
left/to go 4 they pay me back
immediately/I be paid back immediately
5 apply/should apply for it 6 be/was told
7 he passed his test

Unit 34

A 2 shaving/while shaving 3 playing tennis
4 Feeling tired/Yawning 5 Not having
any/Having no

B 2 working 3 Having been 4 not having
met 5 reaching 6 driving 7 being

C 2 introducing himself, the visitor asked
3 Having seen/On seeing a huge savage
dog, Sir Charles (had) died 4 agreeing to
take the case, Holmes asked Watson to
travel to 6 not being a detective, when
Watson arrived 7 knowing Holmes was
also in the area, he tried to solve the
crime himself

D 2 qualifying/having qualified as a doctor,
in 1891 he became 3 being a scientist by
training, he believed in fairies
4 writing/having written several stories
about Sherlock Holmes, in 1893 Conan
Doyle decided 5 returning to England
from South Africa in 1902, he wrote

Unit 35

A 2 as if/though we'd lost 3 as if (though)
to say 4 as if/though I were 5 as
if/though trying (to try) 6 as if/though
they were having 7 as if/though
confused

B Answers will vary. 2 frightened of
something 3 I were crazy/to say you
think I'm crazy 4 there's no-one home
5 I've got a cold/I haven't slept for days
6 (he were) going to a funeral 7 to go
8 seeing herself for the first time

Unit 36

A 2 Located by the River Thames, the
London Eye 3 First launched in 1869,
the *Cutty Sark* is now 4 Originally built
as a prison, the London Dungeon is now
5 Used for important state occasions, the
Crown Jewels are on display

B 2 paid for in advance, tickets for West
End shows can be 3 lost, tourists should
try to find 4 seen, the view from
Waterloo Bridge

Unit 37

A 2 would be; 'd restructured 3 were; 'd
have gone 4 'd invested;
would/might/could be making 5 would
still be working; hadn't made 6 hadn't
lost; 'd still be

B 2 I'd trusted him, we'd be working
3 hadn't gone into business when I was
very young, I wouldn't be 4 I weren't
well-off, I wouldn't have been able to
buy 5 I hadn't been brought up in a
business environment, I wouldn't
understand

Unit 38

A 2 did I climb/had I climbed inside 3 had
I expected/did I expect 4 have/had I
been 5 did the cave get 6 did I feel
7 do I realise

B 2 Never in my life have I been so scared.
3 Under no circumstances should I have
gone in there. 4 Not only will I go with
another person in future but I will also
make sure the cave is safe first. 5 Never
again will I be so silly!

Unit 39

A 2 wanted to discover was/wanted to do
was discover 3 did was fly a kite with a
wire and key attached 4 that happened
was that bits of string 5 happened was
that a spark flew 6 had proved was that
lightning and electricity

B 2 d 3 a 4 e 5 c

C 2 throughout Asia Minor that he travelled widely 3 Cicero who called him the 'father of history' 4 in c460 that he was born 5 Herodotus who is still widely read today 6 in *Hellenica* that he wrote about the Athens-Sparta war

D Answers will vary.

Unit 40

A 2 was her anxiety 3 terrible was the storm 4 was the chaos on the streets 5 unsure was she of her safety/unsure of her safety was she

B 2 The door suddenly opened and out rushed a crazy dog. 3 Waiting for me in the cafe was someone I recognised. 4 The worst thing of all was knowing that he used to be my best friend.

Test 4 (Units 31–40)

A 1 In addition to 2 isn't 3 not be given 4 feeling 5 to show 6 swallowed 7 hadn't been 8 have I seen 9 happened next was 10 hot was it

B 1 has been 2 are climbing/have climbed 3 changed 4 Taking off/Having taken off 5 feeling 6 had happened (was happening) 7 trying 8 Lost 9 didn't live 10 did he ever thank

C 1 so; one 2 Besides 3 What 4 It 5 thing

D 1 While some people look forward to retirement, others can't …/Some people look forward to retirement, while others … 2 As well as helping people in need, the organisation also …/The organisation helps people in need as well as raising … 3 Not having a ticket, I couldn't get …/ I couldn't get into the concert, not having … 4 After living in London, Cambridge seems …/Cambridge seems very quiet to me after living … 5 Despite not doing a very good job, he is paid …/Despite the fact that he doesn't do a very good job, he is paid …/Despite being paid a lot of money, he doesn't do a very good job.

E 1 people should be put in prison 2 meeting, the two men shook hands 3 I hadn't eaten so much, I wouldn't be feeling so ill 4 I weren't good at my job, I wouldn't have got promoted 5 had we arrived than/when the trouble started 6 is he always late but he's (also) very lazy/is he very lazy but 7 he did was take a lot more exercise 8 was when he was on holiday that they met 9 more difficult was the last question 10 was his strength that he could pull a bus

F 1 do 2 isn't 3 to go 4 I sat with my dog 5 he knew 6 opened 7 hadn't said 8 did I find out 9 The person who 10 was a cheque

Acknowledgements

I would particularly like to thank Alison Sharpe for her help, guidance and support during the editing of this series. My thanks also to Jessica Roberts for her expert editing of the material and to Kamae Design and Nick Schon for their excellent design and artwork.

The publisher would like to thank the following for permission to reproduce photographs:

p. 22 Zedda Ivan/Sygma/Corbis, p. 25 Patrick Bennett/Corbis, p. 26 Corbis, p. 28 Parrot Pascal/Sygma/Corbis, p. 31 J. P. Laffont/Sygma/Corbis, p. 32 Bettman/ Corbis, p. 39 Bettman/Corbis, p. 54 Morton Beebe/Corbis, p. 59 E. O. Hoppe/ Corbis, p. 61 London Aerial Photo Library/Sandy Stockwell/Corbis; p. 55 PA/ Empics; p. 5 Bruno Vincent/Getty Images Entertainment, p. 7 David Schlabowske/ Time Life Pictures/Getty Images, p. 13 Tim Graham/Getty Images, p. 14 Getty Images, p. 15 R. McPhedran/Getty Images, p. 39 Martine Mouchy/Photographer's Choice/Getty Images, p. 65 Time Life Pictures/Getty Images; p. 29 20th Century Fox/The Kobal Collection; p. 17 Sideways [US 2004] a Fox Searchlight picture/ The Ronald Grant Archive, p. 53 Chitty Chitty Bang Bang [Br 1968] A United Artists film/The Ronald Grant Archive

Every effort has been made to reach the copyright holders; the publishers would be pleased to hear from anyone whose rights they have unknowingly infringed.

Produced by Kamae Design, Oxford.

Illustrations by Nick Schon.

nce picture research by Geri May.